Moving the Furniture

Liturgical Theory, Practice, and Environment

William Seth Adams

 CHURCH

Church Publishing Incorporated, New York

Library of Congress Cataloging in Publication Data

Adams, William Seth.
  Moving the furniture : liturgical theory, practice, and
environment / William Seth Adams.
     p.   cm.
  Includes bibliographical references.
  ISBN 0-89869-316-0 (pbk.)
  1. Episcopal Church—Liturgy. I. Title.
BX5940.A33 1999
264′.03—dc21
                                              99–22884
                                                 CIP

Church Publishing Incorporated
445 Fifth Avenue
New York, NY 10016

5 4 3 2 1

Table of Contents

Photography by William Seth Adams. Additional photographers: Bob Kinney, page 87, Rick Williams, page 55, and unknown, page 69.

Foreword

What have we here? Quite the right question. This is a collection of essays written over a period of some fifteen years, material embedded in the experience of seminary teaching and nourished by parochial participation. That is, although I served as a parish priest for eight years before beginning a life of teaching, I have spent the last twenty-four years as a professor of liturgical studies. During that time, I have also been a generally active and engaged member of several parish congregations. I am confident that the reader will see evidence of both of these existential informants in what follows.

The title of this collection, *Moving the Furniture,* intends to signal the fact that in virtually every case, and without reference to their individual content, these articles intend to "move the furniture" of the current liturgical situation into some new configuration. They were written and are offered with the intent of changing liturgical opinion and practice.

In preparing these essays for publication as a collection, I have discovered a number of themes that run through them. Some of these themes, of course, determine the organization of this volume and the naming of the subsections—liturgical theory, liturgical practice and liturgical environment. Yet, there are other themes as well, themes to which I might call attention.

The first theme is the frequently considered matter of the ministry of the baptized. This is a central concern in some of the pieces gathered here but it seems to arise in one way or another in nearly all the essays. I am not surprised to find this to be so. Indeed, and to speak frankly, I am reassured by this discovery. Given my disposition, I would want that to be true. In the essays where the ministry or liturgical circumstances of the baptized are of central concern, I discover a certain insufficiency in what the essays have accomplished. That is, since I rather naively think that what the essays have to say ought to change the view or behavior of the church—and I find that the view or behavior of the church has *not* changed—I am disappointed in the extent to which things needful of change have remained the same.

A second theme, almost as common as the first, is that of justice. Here again, this is the central issue in at least one of these essays—that on emancipatory language—but it surfaces not infrequently in others as well. This, too, does not surprise me. I remain hopeful that the church will awaken continuously to the intimate and compelling relationship between justice, on the one hand, and the liturgical and sacramental life, on the other.

The third theme, if it be that, is the conviction that the liturgical life of the church is formative of the life and spirit of the church; indeed, formative of the church itself, in a way. I am beset by the notion that the way we pray together, serve together, eat and drink together—that all this is formative of our heart and life in and for the world.

Almost all of these essays were written before the publication in 1995 of *Shaped by Images: One who Presides.* Any reader of that book will find echoes of it in the current collection. For whatever appropriate continuity there is in this, I am pleased and grateful. At the same time, I freely admit that there are things in the essays in this collection and in *Shaped by Images* about which I have had second or third thoughts. I will report perhaps two of these in the Afterword. (Such admissions should come after the reader has read the essays, not before!)

For some years I have used these essays in my own teaching and have wished that they might be gathered to make that use more convenient for me and for those with whom I study. I hope others will find this useful as well. I am consequently very grateful to Frank Hemlin and Frank Tedeschi of Church Publishing for their interest in this enterprise. I also extend my gratitude (again) to Bob Kinney, who designed this volume and *Shaped by Images.* His care and imagination are in evidence in every visual aspect of the book.

Although she was not with me for all the years during which most of these essays were written, she is now—and I am ever so glad! She is Amy Donohue-Adams. With the rest of the world, she is priest and chaplain. With me, she is lover, companion and friend. To her my great thanks.

William Seth Adams
The Episcopal Theological Seminary of the Southwest
Austin, Texas

February, 1999

Part One

Thinking Something Different

Chapter One

Christian Liturgy, Scripture and the Jews
A Problematic in Jewish-Christian Relations[1]

T he increasing ease with which Christians and Jews think, talk and even pray together needs to be a cause for resounding joy among the churches. It is a hopeful and reconciling sign. Unfortunately, at least in

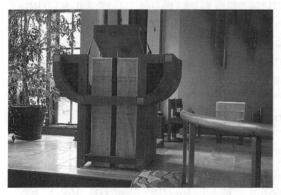

some instances, the ritual life of the church may not foster this reconciliation. It may in fact work against it. This thought set this article in motion.

The concern of this essay is the connection between the history and practice of Christian liturgy and the Jews. There are two sides to the matter. Firstly, there is the matter of origins of Christian ritual practice in the ritual of the Jews. Secondly, there is the matter of the impact of Christian ritual practice on the attitude of Christians toward Jews. Of these two issues, origins and impact, the latter is the more important for the moment and will receive the greater exploration. This exploration, however, does not lead to conclusion so much as to dilemma, the "problematic" in the sub-title. Sadly, the resolution of the dilemma exceeds the limits of the writer's imagination, for which apologies are offered at the outset.

Origins

The human spirit requires ritual. The stories we tell, the myths that shape us and give us meaning need to be acted out. The human communities that people the earth (now and always) need their "corporate symbolic activity" to give themselves identity.[2] This fact about the human condition is clearly the first "source" for Christian liturgical practice. That Christians have a meal and a ritual bath at the center of their liturgy is predictable. It is what people do; what people value; what people need in order to live. That Christians mark time with calendars peculiar to themselves is also predictable. Timekeeping is identity giving. That Christian ritualizing is patterned and archaic is likewise predictable. Rituals are formal and conservative of the past, stylized in some measure and, consequently, highly charged with collected and complicated meanings. That Christians mark crises in life and seasonal changes with ritual observations is not surprising either and needs little explanation beyond what one learns observing "how folks are."

This being so, it seems initially odd to read the following, "When . . . the question is asked against what background Christian worship arose, the only answer that can be given is Jewish worship."[3] Nonsense! It may be true that the proximate background for the Church's ritual life is first century Judaism but surely the larger, more fundamental human setting warrants at least a mention. Both Christians and Jews ritualize as they do because that is what religious people do.

That point being made well enough for the moment, the "proximate background" now needs attention. Meals, washings, time, patterns for prayer, acclamations, poetry—these Christians evolved into unique forms or adopted without alteration from their forebears. We will consider some of them briefly in turn. The meal tradition among the people of Israel is and was strong, and Christian "ritual indebtedness" to that tradition is obviously deep.[4] The subtleties of the development from Passover observance to Eucharist cannot detain us here but the following are worth noting. (1) The meal community of which Jesus was a part was the community of the upper room. To them he directed that they "do this" for his remembrance. What they were to do was to gather, bless bread and wine, and share in it, as they had no doubt done many times before. In eating together, they were to remember until they were together again. (2) The pattern of blessing which grew in the church for this meal was likely derived from the table blessings of the Jews, *Birkat ha-Mazon*. An example of this threefold blessing is as follows:

Blessing of him who nourishes

Blessed are you, Lord our God, King of the universe,
for you nourish us and the whole world
with goodness, grace, kindness, and mercy.
Blessed are you, Lord, for you nourish the
universe.

Blessing for the earth

We will give thanks to you, Lord our God,
because you have given us for our inheritance a
desirable land, good and wide, the covenant and
the Law, life and food. And for all these
things we give you thanks and bless your name
for ever and beyond.
Blessed are you, Lord our God, for the earth and for food.

Blessing for Jerusalem

Have mercy, Lord our God, on us your people
Israel, and your city Jerusalem, on your
sanctuary and your dwelling place, on Zion the
habitation of your glory, and the great and holy
house over which your name is invoked. Restore
the kingdom of the house of David to its place
in our days, and speedily build Jerusalem.
Blessed are you, Lord, for you build Jerusalem. Amen.[5]

The *Didache* (early second century CE) and the prayers found in the *Apostolic Tradition* of Hippolytus (ca. 215 CE) would show development beyond this pattern.

If the meal aspect of the church's common liturgy takes its proximate origins from the meal tradition of the Jews, the liturgy of the word appears to draw on the daily private prayers of the devout Jew as those prayers found expression in the Synagogue, the same point of origin for the daily office. Paul Bradshaw, writing in *Daily Prayer in the Early Church,* observes that it is likely that the liturgical pattern for first century Jews would have included (1) private daily prayers—morning, midday and evening—perhaps said corporately in the synagogue in larger cities;[6] and (2) regular Synagogue services on the Sabbath, Monday and Thursday. These would have included the *Shema* ["Hear, O Israel, the Lord our God, the Lord alone . . ." Deut 6.4f] and *Tefillah* (prayers) along with a reading from the Books of Moses and, on the Sabbath, a reading from the Prophets as well. Following the reading, an exposition would likely be given.[7] The transference of this pattern to Sunday, Wednesday and Friday by Christians by the end of the first century may have been due to the influence of another sect of Judeans, the community at Qumran, in which these days had particular standing.[8] This service of prayer and readings was combined with the meal liturgy on Sunday, a day whose importance for Christians was obviously independent of the influence of Qumran.[9]

Thus, into the emerging Christian context were taken a collection of patterns at work in the first century setting, a collection out of which later Judaism would also fashion its liturgy.

Predictably, time keeping in the earliest community followed the patterns that were natural to it. That is, to the extent that Christians were sectarian Jews, the pattern of the Jews predominate. The translation of Passover and Pentecost into Christian feasts was an evolutionary process, accomplished in large measure by the end of the second century. The Great Fifty Days, that time between Passover and Pentecost, emerged as the first great season of the church.[10] Likewise, the seven-day ordering of the week came directly from the Jews as well, the first day being the Christian's special day. It is worth noting, at the same time, that as late as the fourth century, some Christians were still observing both *Shabat* and the Lord's Day.[11] That this was true in Antioch drew some of the most vitriolic language from John Chrysostom.[12]

The Didachist, writing perhaps at the turn of the first century of the common era, admonished his readers to fast on Wednesday and Friday (*Didache* 8). The text suggests that these days were to be used rather than Monday and Thursday, the fast days of the "hypocrites." This may be a direct reference to the practice of the Jews or to those who advocated Jewish observance for Christians. It may also represent a point of view from within the community of Jewish Christians, arguing over traditional fast days and those exemplified in the Qumran community.[13] The evolution of Christian ritual washing (baptism) is complicated. Aidan Kavanaugh's summary will serve the purposes of this essay. Early Christian practice is best understood as a synthesis of perhaps three strands: Jewish proselyte baptism which was coming to have both purificatory and initiatory aspects, the ablutions of the more ascetical Jewish sects (Qumran, for example) and the prophetic eschatological expectations associated with the baptism offered by John the Baptizer.[14] These associations, however diverse, would place the Christian sect of Jews rather toward the edge of normative practice but still rightly within the full spectrum of first century alternatives.

That Christians took into their ritual practice "technical terms" such as Amen, Hallelujah, and Hosanna is common knowledge and that the Psalms of the Hebrew Scriptures became a basic part of Christian liturgy is easily admitted. And, indeed, there are other points one might make which would extend this list even further. Yet for our purposes, it seems clear enough the extent to which the ritual life of the Jews served as a primary context for the fashioning of Christian ritual practice. It is also clear in some measure the extent to which the *compatibility* of the one with the other was taken for granted. It is around this last point that changes one might expect were to occur. Charting these changes is basic to the later part of these remarks.

Consequences of Self-definition

Self-definition became a central concern for the Jews by the later part of the first century of the common era and earlier for the Christians. In some measure, this process of self-definition was worked out against the surrounding Roman culture and in some measure it was worked out vis-à-vis each other. This latter is particularly true of the Christians.

As the church emerged into Mediterranean history, one sees it seemingly striving to discover norms and standards by which to organize and identify itself. These norms, expressions of "the principle of canonicity" as Reginald Fuller has called it,[15] were three: authoritative writings, authoritative leadership and authoritative doctrine. The New Testament was the first, the ordered ministry the second and the emergence of orthodoxy in the form of the apostolic tradition the third. Primary characteristics of this process of norm-setting were the "need for uniformity and homogeneity, a need to outlaw deviance from [the church's] communion as 'heresy' and an inability to preserve the ecumenicity of diverse traditions."[16]

This being so, within the development of the New Testament and in the formation of an authoritative body of theological teachings, one sees the church expressing, on the one hand, its theological commitment to proclaim Jesus "Lord" and, on the other, its sociological or organizational need to define itself vis-à-vis the Jews. Eventually, the combination of these two factors led to strong language of condemnation of the Jews and the creation of the *Adversus Judaeos* tradition. We can best illustrate this point with the insights of Rosemary Ruether and John Gager.[17] And please note, the illustrations are the extreme case. Perhaps the most profound scriptural example of this combination of factors is found in John's Gospel. "Throughout, the author uses 'the Jews' universally and without internal distinction as a synonym for the opponents of Jesus. He holds to a replacement theory in which Israel no longer has any but a negative status before God."[18]

The denigration of the Jews in John's Gospel is best exemplified perhaps in John 8:44, where Jesus responds to the Pharisees who have laid claim to being the children of Abraham. Jesus, in John, says, "You are of your father the devil; and your will is to do your father's desires." This statement needs to be added to the several occasions on which Jesus is heard to say that the Jews have never known God or are unrelated to

Christian Liturgy, Scripture and the Jews

God, one of which examples follows almost immediately on the charge of being children of the Devil (John 8:47; see also 8:19, 15:21, 16:3).

The most difficult aspect of John's treatment of the Jews is his account of the crucifixion. Rosemary Ruether writes,

> John goes farthest of all the Gospels in depicting Jesus as actually being crucified *by the Jews* . . . for John, it is crucial that Jesus be crucified, not by the Romans as a political dissident, but by the Jewish religious authorities for the religious crime of blasphemy. This means that the One who is the unique revelation of God in the world, God's very self-manifestation . . . is killed by the Jews as an explicit rejection by them of this divine identity. Thus John moves the 'crime of the Jews' very close to what will become the charge of 'deicide,' i.e., that 'the Jews', in killing Jesus, commit the religious crime of rejection and murder, not merely of God's prophet, but of God's revealed self-expression.[19]

In addition to such examples from the New Testament writings, the other aspect of the expression of Christian self-definition is the *Adversus Judaeos* literature, mentioned earlier, presumably so named after a treatise by that name written by Tertullian. This complex body of literature is composed of dialogues between Christians and Jews, e.g., Justin's *Dialogue with Trypho the Jew*, treatises like Tertullian's (and that called *Expository Treatise against the Jews*, attributed to Hippolytus, and Augustine's *Tractatus Adversus Judaeos*), and collections called "testimonies" which were actually lists of proof texts gathered under assorted headings designed to illustrate the rejection of the Jews (e.g., Cyprian's *The Three Books of Testimonies Against the Jews*).[20]

To these literary sources one would need to add homiletical sources. The most pungent example must certainly be the oratory of John Chrysostom, who described the community of the synagogue in fourth century Antioch as "the fellowship of the Christ-killers."[21] It is perhaps ironic to note that Chrysostom's vitriol was occasioned by the apparent attraction the local Jewish congregation had for Christians.[22] Growing out of at least some of the views expressed in the New Testament, the

Adversus Judaeos literature seems to have contributed significantly to the post-Constantinian legislation (4th century onward) which eventually reduced Jews to virtual prisoners of Europe by the 13th century. The emancipation of the Jews in France in 1791 may perhaps mark the end of what one author has called the 'Christian religious totalitarianism' set in motion by this anti-Jewish legislation.[23]

Liturgical Formation and Liturgical History

To this point we have explored in some small measure the rootedness of Christian liturgy in its Jewish developmental setting and touched on the anti-Jewish side of the Church's efforts at self-definition. These efforts, we suggested, found expression in law (and social custom, for that matter). Now it is time to look again at the liturgy.

The premise which will be developed from this point onward is that Christian ritualization has in the past overtly fostered Christian anti-Semitism and, though greatly reformed in our day, still carries this possibility within it. This view is, in turn, based on the assumption that the practice of Christian liturgy is formative of the life of the Church.

In the recent book called *The Service of God*, subtitled "How Worship and Ethics are Related," William Willimon, a Methodist professor at Duke Divinity School, has enumerated ways in which the liturgy serves as a place for the formation of Christian character. The six ways are as follows:

> Liturgy helps form Christian identity.
> Liturgy creates a world for the Christian.
> Liturgy is a primary source of the symbols and metaphors through which Christians talk about and make sense out of our world.
> Liturgy aids in Christian imagination.
> Liturgy is a primary source of the Christian vision.
> Liturgy is a major source of the Christian tradition which enables the church to rise above the present and envision a future.[24]

Similarly, Christopher Kiesling, writing on "The Formative Influence of Liturgy," speaks of the persistent and subtle but deep and real influence liturgical participation exerts, particularly through the keeping of the liturgical year.[25]

What makes the insights of Willimon and Kiesling accurate and valuable is that they are describing the way in which rituals work. Rituals provide memory, identity and community-vision for their participants. What is *expressed* in the ritual is *impressed* upon the participants. Indeed, this conviction needs extension. That is, it can be argued that the formative influence is more powerful the more central the ritual to the life of the community. Christian theology/Christian meaning is expressed and Christians are fashioned in the liturgy. This premise informs our perspective and is basic to what follows.

Earlier we admitted that in citing John's Gospel and the *Adversus Judaeos* tradition we were citing the extreme case. The same admission might be made at this point as well since we are choosing a particular liturgical situation in order to illustrate what may rightly be called "liturgical anti-Judaism."[26] The particular liturgical situation is Holy Week.

Holy Week is a product of the 4th century pilgrim church in Jerusalem. It appears in full expression by the 380's. We know this because we possess a wonderful account from a woman, perhaps Spanish, named Egeria.[27] *Egeria's Travels* tells us about the historicization of the events of the Passion. The events were first attached to the days of the week on which they occurred in the gospel narratives, and then enacted in the spot where they reportedly happened. It could only happen in Jerusalem!

The interest in history evidenced in this historicization was clearly not available to the church during its eschatological period nor was it an option so long as the church saw itself as standing over against the world. "The abandonment of this anti-historical attitude could take place only with the cessation of hostility between the Church and the secular society, and this indeed was the immediate result of the conversion of Constantine."[28] The practical result was the historicizing of the process of redemption, allowing "the Church's Calendar to develop into a series of historical commemorations."[29]

This is certainly clear from Egeria's account. Every detail of the week's events is observed. On Friday we are told of a three-hour service—midday to three o'clock—composed of readings and prayers. Egeria's description is important:

> It is impressive to see the way all the people are moved by these readings, and how they mourn. You could hardly believe how every single one of them weeps during the three hours, old and young alike, because of the manner in which the Lord suffered for us. Then when three o'clock comes, they have the reading from St. John's Gospel about Jesus giving up the ghost, and when that has been read, there is a prayer, and the dismissal.[30]

Surely it is no exaggeration to expect this experience to be formative of the people's spirituality. Imagine, an observance of the Day of Crucifixion in the Holy City culminating in a final reading from John's Gospel. And all this within some few years of the Emperor Theodosius's public declaration in favor of Catholic Christianity and the outlawing of paganism! Although Jews were not outlawed, their status as "reprobates" was working its way increasingly into legislation.[31]

Once Holy Week as such existed, it spread throughout the church so that probably not later than the 9th century it was a fairly common observance, though its means of observance was far from uniform.[32] As Holy Week spread, we find two additions to the Holy Week liturgy of particular importance to our topic, both additions again a part of the Good Friday observance. These are the Solemn Prayers or Collects and the Reproaches.

Dating from perhaps as early as the 5th century,[33] the Solemn Prayers are a series of nine intercessory prayers which follow immediately the reading of the Good Friday Gospel, John 18 and 19.[34] Prayer is offered for the whole church, the Pope, all Christians, the Sovereign, catechumens, the world, heretics and schismatics, Jews and lastly heathen. With one exception, the pattern for these prayers is the same: the priest bids prayers for those appointed, the deacon says for all to kneel, silent prayer follows, the subdeacon says for all to rise, and the priest offers a collect to which all respond "Amen."

The exception to this pattern is the petition for the Jews. Whereas even the schismatics and heathen are prayed for with kindness and hope, the Jews "are branded with the epithet *perfidi* ('faithless'); surprise is almost expressed that God does not regard them as beyond recovery . . . ; and in most rites they are not considered worth silent prayer." No invitation to kneel or arise is given.[35]

The Reproaches occur later in the liturgy, as part of the Veneration of the Cross. Dating from perhaps the 8th century,[36] the Reproaches are cast as rebukes of the people Israel by the crucified Christ; one common source says they "set in parallel the Divine compassion for Israel and the outrage inflicted on Christ in His Passion."[37]

Following the unveiling of the cross and acts of veneration such as kissings and prostrations, the priest begins the exchange, the people or more likely the choir responding. As an example, the first Reproach reads, "O my people, what have I done to thee, or wherein have I saddened thee? Answer me. Because I brought thee out of the land of Egypt, thou hast prepared a cross for thy Savior." The response is the Trisagion, "Holy God, Holy and Mighty, Holy and Immortal, have mercy on us." This pattern applies to the first three Reproaches, the remaining nine being sung without the Trisagion.

It became common practice for the Reproaches to be sung by two choirs, preferably set at different points in the building so that the verses and responses would have a kind of antiphonal power and enshroud the acts of veneration. A very powerful scene, no doubt!

One finds then a kind of accumulation. From the events presented in the Gospels comes the *theological* testimony about the end of Jesus' life. The historicization of the events of the capture and crucifixion of Jesus emerge by the 4th century as Holy Week. Into this observance are introduced liturgical acts and language of obvious anti-Semitic content. To these one need only add the increasingly dramatic, allegorical presentation and interpretation of the Mass and the translation of that allegorical drama into popular performance, the Passion Plays and Prophet Plays,[38] and one has no difficulty in seeing the dissemination of anti-Jewish sentiment inspired by and rooted in the scriptural and theological convictions of the church and taught in its ritual/liturgical activities.

Vamberto Morais recounts the following detail. By the 13th century the round of plays and liturgical observances made "the drama of the Passion . . . an integral part of Christian life." In them the depiction of the Jews was such that, to cite but one example, priests in the city of Beziers, in the south of France, are reported to have given this charge to the faithful at the beginning of Holy Week:

> You have around you those who crucified this Messiah, who deny Mary the Mother of God. Now is the time when you would feel most deeply the iniquity of which Christ was the victim. This is the day on which our Prince has graciously given us permission to avenge this crime. Like your pious ancestors, hurl stones at the Jews, and show your sense of his wrongs by the vigour with which you resent them.

Morais concludes his story by saying that interference with such practices by bishops often issued in charges suggesting that the bishop had been bribed by the Jews.[39] The historical reality of Christian anti-Semitism is there to be seen. The contention of this essay is that it is intimately related to Christian ritual practice.

Current Liturgical Practice

Our own time and experience benefit from what we know of our past. Some of what we have pointed to from the past has been changed, to the good and, one hopes, for good. We will identify those as a way to begin to describe what is the nature of the liturgy's current impact on the relations of Christians and Jews.

The Solemn Prayers and the Reproaches remain in the Roman rite to the present. As regards the latter, they remain, in our view, anti-Semitic and are therefore unacceptable. We are assured by those who have experienced them for years that they are *not* heard as speaking against the Jews but are rather heard as against sinful humanity. We can accept this claim for those who make it yet surely some other way can be found to accomplish this without citing exclusively the failure of the Jews to perform all righteousness.[40]

In the Solemn Prayers, the petition regarding the Jews has been changed significantly. Firstly, the posture for the prayers is uniform for all of them. Secondly, instead of speaking for the repudiation of the Jews or for their conversion, the people are invited to pray "for the Jewish people the first to hear the word of God, that they may continue to grow in the love of his name and in faithfulness to his covenant." After that bidding, the prayer itself contains this petition, "Listen to your Church as we pray that the people you first made your own may arrive at the fullness of redemption."[41] We take this last to mean that the Church prays that God will fulfill God's promises to the Chosen People, i.e., "the fullness of redemption." This is quite a change from the prayer built around the 'perfidious' Jews.

The *Lutheran Book of Worship* does not contain the Reproaches in any form but it virtually duplicates the current Roman form of the Solemn Collects. The LBW, of course, does not contain the prayer for the Pope. It concludes with the Lord's Prayer.[42]

Anglican rites have never contained the Reproaches although they were *almost* part of the current revision of the Book of Common Prayer.[43] Forms of the Reproaches, however, have been readily available, not only from Roman Catholic sources but also from unofficial Episcopal Church sources, e.g., the *Holy Week Offices* produced by the Associated Parishes.[44] More recently they have been published in Dennis Michno's *A Priest's Handbook*.[45] Michno argues that although they have been identified as anti-Semitic, they can nonetheless be used if adequate teaching is done.[46]

In addition to the Reproaches and Solemn Collects, the church's Holy Week legacy includes the Scriptures, especially in this case the Johannine readings. Although in broad terms, things are not as they have been, all is finally not well.

On the matter of biblical education and interpretation, our time is greatly enriched. Our understanding of the world of the first Christians allows us to bring new and helpful perspectives to the reading and preaching of the New Testament. We are more able, for example, to see Jesus' debates with the Pharisees as something akin to an intramural sport rather than as arguments between forces of 'good' and 'evil.' As we come to a clearer sense of the nature of first century Judaism, a place is found within it for this sect called Christians.[47]

This historical perspective is helpful in dealing with the problem posed in the Good Friday liturgy by the persistent annual reading of the Passion from John. It is this gospel which is the traditional reading for this occasion[48] and, as was suggested earlier, it is the most likely to be accused of anti-Jewish bias.[49]

We are helped in our reaction to hearing John's Passion Narrative by knowing that "there are indications in the text that the gospel grew out of local tensions between John's community and a local synagogue," that "the Johannine community came into being as a distinct entity only after being expelled, as a group, from a Jewish community."[50] This helps to account for the fact that John has a penchant for naming the "bad guys" in his story "the Jews" instead of "the crowd," "the leaders of the people," "some of the people," or even "the religious leaders who collaborated with the Roman occupation."

We are also aided by the clarity with which scholars have shown that Jesus was killed by the Roman occupation forces as a political act against a person perceived as a political enemy, "an insurrectionist" as it were.[51]

Yet, although we are aided by the insights of critical scholarship, it does not really solve the problem. And in saying that, we approach the first aspect of the dilemma promised at the outset. The dilemma is put thusly by John Townsend, Professor of New Testament at the Episcopal Divinity School:

> Understanding why the New Testament is often anti-Jewish does not excuse us from removing the effects of such anti-Jewishness today. Leaving aside the question of Scripture and historical accuracy, one can hardly deny that the public reading of certain New Testament passages perpetuates distorted views of our Jewish neighbors.

We should not continue to broadcast such views before congregations who are generally ready to accept Scripture quite uncritically. The problem of such reading is not going to be resolved by new translations. The anti-Jewish passages within the New Testament are extensive enough (that) to "translate" them out would involve the complete rewriting of much that we hold sacred.

Townsend continues:

A particular problem surrounds the Holy Week services in most churches. It is both customary and fitting to read about our Lord's Passion at this time. Unfortunately the Passion narratives contain some of the most pronounced anti-Jewish parts of the New Testament. They all place the primary responsibility for the crucifixion squarely on the Jews, and one cannot avoid this distortion of what actually took place through any editing of a minor nature.[52]

Townsend's "solution" is *A Liturgical Interpretation of Our Lord's Passion in Narrative Form.* This admirable document is designed to be a liturgical re-casting of the Passion, based largely on Matthew and Mark, yet not presenting either directly. As a warrant for this idea, Townsend cites the fact that the story of the Last Supper contained in the eucharistic prayers of the churches follows no one biblical account but rather is an amalgam.[53] The author intends the *Interpretation* to be used *in place of* the gospel readings appointed.

For Episcopalians, at least, and presumably for other Christians who are similarly obligated to liturgical rubrics, the difficulty with this solution is that such substitution is not sanctioned, anywhere, by anyone in authority. The Prayer Book obliges the reading of the Gospel at every eucharist, without exception. As a study and teaching document Townsend's *Interpretation* is very powerful (and properly edifying) but it simply cannot serve "legally" as a replacement for what the *lectionary* requires.

So, the puzzle remains. What to do with the anti-Jewish language and point of view found some places in the New Testament read regularly in the church's liturgy, the liturgy that forms the church? That is the first part of the dilemma, made explicit in the Holy Week observances. As Townsend has said, the church cannot simply re-write something "we hold sacred."[54]

We need now to move away from our preoccupation with Holy Week and to turn instead to the regular liturgical life of the church. This setting will serve to illustrate the other, equally nettlesome part of our dilemma. In order to set the stage for further inquiry, however, two observations are needful.

First, as we mentioned earlier, there is a growing number of Christian scholars who would join Jewish scholars in *rejecting* the notion that God's actions in Jesus brought an end to the validity of God's covenant with the Jews. That is, there are those who suggest that we are *mislead* if we claim that Christians replace or supersede the Jews as God's Chosen. John Pawlikowski does everyone a service by cataloging these views in his *Christ in the Light of Christian-Jewish Dialogue,*[55] though he leaves out the important work of Lloyd Gaston on Paul.[56]

If this view is correct, then what does it mean for the church's theology and liturgical language to assert that the covenant God made with the People Israel on Sinai remains valid, and has not been superseded or re-placed? What does it do to the church's understanding of atonement, for example, or its view toward the "conversion" of Jews as a part of the Christian evangelizing?

The second observation is this: it was once true that the language of the church's eucharistic praying was the most basic language of Christian faith and theology. What was believed was re-capitulated in the Great Thanksgiving. That priority was perhaps challenged by the accession of the creeds to a place in regular public worship. Now, however, it seems true that something of that earlier spirit is returning to the churches as new prayer formulas are fashioned for eucharistic praying.

During a visit to the Episcopal Seminary in Austin, Texas, Henry Chadwick, the Oxford historian, in casual conversation with the faculty, was heard to say that he thought that Eucharistic Prayer B in the American Book of Common Prayer was probably the best one such he knew.

We choose it then as our sample from the regular liturgy (of the Episcopal Church), and thus move beyond the "worst case" character of previous examples. (It should also be noted that although this prayer formula originates in the Episcopal Church, the observations which follow will find expression in the texts of other churches.)

Following the opening dialogue, the preface for the day and the Sanctus ("Holy, Holy, Holy Lord, etc."), the text continues,

> We give thanks to you, O God, for the goodness and love which you have made known to us in creation; in the calling of Israel to be your people; in your Word spoken through the prophets; and above all the in the Word made flesh, Jesus, your Son. For in these last days you sent him to be incarnate from the Virgin Mary, to be the Savior and Redeemer of the world. In him, you have delivered us from evil, and made us worthy to stand before you. In him, you have brought us out of error into truth, out of sin into righteousness, out of death into life.

> On the night before he died for us, our Lord Jesus Christ took bread; and when he had given thanks to you, he broke it, and gave it to his disciples, and said, "Take, eat: This is my Body, which is given for you. Do this for the remembrance of me."

> After supper he took the cup of wine; and when he had given thanks, he gave it to them, and said, "Drink this, all of you: This is my Blood of the new Covenant, which is shed for you and for many for the forgiveness of sins. Whenever you drink it, do this for the remembrance of me."

> Therefore, according to his command, O Father,

> We remember his death,
> We proclaim his resurrection,
> We await his coming in glory;

> And we offer our sacrifice of praise and thanksgiving to you, O Lord of all; presenting to you, from your creation, this bread and wine.

We pray you, gracious God, to send your Holy Spirit upon these gifts that they may be the Sacrament of the Body of Christ and his Blood of the new Covenant. Unite us to your Son in his sacrifice, that we may be acceptable through him, being sanctified by the Holy Spirit. In the fullness of time, put all things in subjection under your Christ, and bring us to that heavenly country where, with [_____ and] all your saints, we may enter the everlasting heritage of your sons and daughters; through Jesus Christ our Lord, the firstborn of all creation, the head of the Church, and the author of our salvation.

By him, and with him, and in him, in the unity of
the Holy Spirit all honor and glory is yours,
Almighty Father, now and for ever. AMEN.[57]

Now, regarding this text, two observations present themselves in light of the problem under consideration in this essay.

Firstly, at the end of the first paragraph the text says that in Christ God "has brought us out of error into truth, out of sin into righteousness, out of death into life." How is this to be understood? What is the context for error, sin and death? Is this sentence to be viewed historically, suggesting that the early Christians were lead out of the community of the Jews into the "true faith"? Is it to be understood in some private, particularist fashion meaning that before "conversion" each Christian was in error, sin and death but has now been lead from that to truth, righteousness and life? Is "us" here the baptized (i.e., the church), or Gentiles, or the whole world? Certainly there are other ways to read this line, perhaps better alternatives. It is clear, however, that certain combinations lead in directions which would obviously collide with a conviction about God's continued faithfulness to the Jews. One suspects that the literal, i.e., historical, reading is the most common.

Secondly, in the middle of the next to last paragraph, echoing Paul (I Cor 15:27) and the Psalmist (86), the church asks God to "put all things in subjection under your Christ." How is this to be understood? Jews and Christians await the resolution of history, the messianic hope that human sinfulness will be erased, the riddle of the human condition be resolved; that war, famine, savagery and murder will disappear, the times will be redeemed. Is this the messianic hope which the church begs from God in this passage? This would surely be consistent with the prayer of the Jews who also hope and pray for such fulfillment. Is the church then able to hope with them, to hope that the one Christians await for the second time is the one the Jews await for the first? Is this what the church means by "subjection under your Christ," or something else? Does the church mean to ask God that the whole world be Christianized? Even in light of our history, if this latter, then what of the Jews? Are they not already intimately related to the God whom Jesus called Father, are they not related *before* the church, are they not "saved" because they "are a people holy to the LORD . . . chosen . . . to be a people of [the LORD's] own possession, out of all the people that are on the face of the earth"? (Deut 7:6)

Behind these considerations of the liturgy and its impact, both now and in the past, lies a growing conviction about God's faithfulness to the covenant made with the Jews. For the author, however, the precipitant giving rise to that conviction is the stark reality of Auschwitz and Christian complicity therein.

John Pawlikowski, to whom we referred earlier, has written that although the Holocaust was

> in the last analysis the product of secular, profoundly anti-Christian forces and not simply the final chapter in the long history of Christian anti-semitism, there is no doubt that traditional Christian anti-semitism provided the indispensable seedbed for the successful implementation of the Nazi "Final Solution." [58]

It is in the knowledge of the truth of this statement that the church's language about "subjection" is particularly difficult.

These two citations from the Episcopal Book of Common Prayer serve to illustrate the problem and the dilemma to some extent. Other examples could be offered but they would only duplicate (or exacerbate) the puzzle already before us, namely, is this ritual language, this theological perspective "forming" the church in such a way as to reconcile the peoples of God . . . or not? That is the question!

So ends our argument. The dilemma we encounter is real and fraught with difficulties. The stumbling block, of course, is the matter of obedience, obedience to the rubrical and canonical judgment of the church, disregard of which would be required in order even to attempt resolution. The author sees no way out, for now.

Perhaps God's perpetual transformation of the church will resolve this in ways yet concealed. The Holy One of Israel has saved the church before. In the meantime, we close with a parenthetical suggestion to the Christians who read this. Late in the month of Nisan in the lunar calendar, many Jews observe *Yom Ha'Shoah*. As a modern observance, *Yom Ha'Shoah* is a day of remembrance for the victims of the Holocaust, the destruction of European Jewry by the Nazis between 1933 and 1945. The suggestion is this: befriend your local rabbi, ask him/her if you might come and 'remember' with the Jews. Doing so, at the very least, may help the church avoid what the late Jules Isaac called "the teaching of contempt."

---

1. An earlier version of these remarks was given as a part of the Blandy Alumni Lectures, the Episcopal Theological Seminary of the Southwest. Readers will quickly discover that the Episcopal Church remains the primary exemplar. At the same time, readers from other Christian churches can perhaps provide their own useful illustrations.

2. Leonel Mitchell, *The Meaning of Ritual* (New York: Paulist Press, 1977), p. xi.

3. Roger Beckwith, "The Jewish Background to Christian Worship" in *The Study of Liturgy,* edited by Cheslyn Jones, Geoffrey Wainwright and Edward Yarnold, S.J. (London: SPCK, 1978), p. 39.

4. S.G. Wilson, "Passover, Easter and Anti-Judaism: Melito of Sardis and Others," unpublished. An interesting treatment of perennial questions is Frank Senn's recent article, "The Lord's Supper, Not the Passover Seder," *Worship* 60/4 (July, 1986).

5. Geoffrey Cuming, *He Gave Thanks: An Introduction to the Eucharistic Prayer* [Grove Liturgical Study No. 28](Bramcote, Notts, UK: Grove Books, 1981), pp. 5–6.

6. (New York: Oxford University Press, 1982), p. 18.

7. *Ibid.*, p. 19.

8. *Ibid.*, p. 41.

9. *Ibid.*, p. 66.

10. Peter Cobb, "The History of the Christian Year," in *The Study of Liturgy*, previously cited, p. 411.

11. C.W. Dugmore, *The Influence of the Synagogue upon the Divine Office* (Oxford University Press, 1945), p. 35.

12. Wayne A. Meeks and Robert L. Wilken, *Jews and Christians in Antioch in the First Four Centuries of the Common Era* (Missoula, MT: Scholar's Press, 1978), p. 30f.

13. This is an extrapolation from a point made by Thomas Talley, "From *Berakah* to *Eucharistia*: A Re-opening Question," *Worship* 50/2 (March, 1976), p. 128.

14. Aidan Kavanaugh, *The Shape of Baptism: The Rite of Christian Initiation* (New York: Pueblo, 1978), pp. 8–11.

15. "The Development of Ministry" in *Lutheran-Episcopal Dialogue: A Progress Report* (Cincinnati, OH: Forward Movement, 1972), p. 81.

16. R.A. Markus, "The Problem of Self-Definition: From Sect to Church" in *Jewish and Christian Self-Definition*, Volume One, *The Shaping of Christianity in the Second and Third Centuries*, ed. by E.P. Sanders (London: SCM, 1980), p. 15.

17. Rosemary Ruether, *Faith and Fratricide: The Theological Roots of Anti-Semitism* (New York: Seabury, 1979), and John Gager, *The Origins of Anti-Semitism* (Oxford and New York: Oxford University Press, 1983).

18. Gager, *Origins,* previously cited, p. 151.

19. *Faith and Fratricide,* previously cited, p. 144.

20. Gager, *Origins,* previously cited, pp. 155–156.

21. Meeks and Wilken, *Jews and Christians in Antioch,* previously cited, p. 31.

22. *Ibid.*, pp. 31–32.

23. Jacob Markus, *The Jews of the Medieval World* (Cincinnati, OH: The Union of American Hebrew Congregations, 1938), p. ix.

24. (Nashville: Abingdon Press, 1983), pp. 48–72.

25. "The Formative Influence of Liturgy," in *Studies in Formative Spirituality*, III/3 (November, 1982), pp. 377–385.

26. Wilson, "Passover, Easter and Anti-Judaism," previously cited, p. 25.

27. *Egeria's Travels*, ed. by John Wilkinson (London: SPCK, 1970).

28. J.G. Davies, *Holy Week: A Short History* [Ecumenical Studies in Worship No. 11] (Richmond, VA: John Knox, 1963), p. 13.

29. *Ibid.*, p. 15.

30. *Egeria's Travels*, previously cited, 37.6.

31. Ruether, *Faith and Fratricide*, previously cited, p. 185f.

32. Davies, *Holy Week*, previously cited, p. 39.

33. John Walton Tyler, *Historical Survey of Holy Week: Its Services and Ceremonial* (London: Oxford University Press, 1932), p. 126.

34. *Ibid.*, p. 66.

35. *Ibid.*, p. 125.

36. So Davies, *Holy Week*, previously cited, p. 51. Behind the Reproaches likely lies Melito of Sardis, as per Eric Werner, "Melito of Sardis, the First Poet of Deicide," in *Hebrew Union College Annual*, Cincinnati, Volume 37, 1966, pp. 191–210. Contrary to Davies, Werner suggests the 7th century, p. 196.

37. *Oxford Dictionary of the Christian Church*, ed. by F.L. Cross and E.A. Livingston (Oxford: Oxford University Press, 1974), p. 1175.

38. Wolfgang S. Seiferth, *Synagogue and Church in the Middle Ages: Two Symbols in Art and Literature* trans. by Lee Chadeayne and Paul Gottwald (New York: Frederick Ungar, 1970), pp. 41, 141ff.

39. *A Short History of Anti-Semitism* (New York: Norton, 1970), pp. 96–97.

40. A United Methodist revision of the Reproaches attempts this with considerable success. *Ashes to Fire* [Supplemental Worship Resources No. 8](Nashville: Abingdon, 1979). The traditional first reproach, "O my people, what have I done to thee, etc." appears as the second in the Methodist rendition and reads, "O my people, O my Church, what have I done to you . . ." The number of reproaches has been expanded and includes the following interesting addition, "I grafted you into the tree of my chosen Israel, and you turned on them with persecution and mass murder. I made you joint heirs with them of my cove-

nants, but you made them scapegoats for your own guilt." Quoted in Dennis Michno, *A Priest's Handbook* (Wilton, CT: Morehouse-Barlow, 1983), p. 259.

41. *The [Roman Catholic] Sacramentary* (Huntington, IN: Our Sunday Visitor, 1974), p. 277.

42. [Minister's Desk Edition](Minneapolis: Augsburg, 1978), pp. 139–142.

43. (New York: Seabury Press and The Church Hymnal Corporation, 1979). See the interesting article by Thomas Idinopulos which explains the "almost." "Old Forms of Anti-Judaism in the New Book of Common Prayer," *Christian Century* XCIII/25 (August 4–11, 1976), pp. 680–684.

44. Edited by Massey Shepherd (Greenville, CT: Seabury, 1958).

45. See Note 40, above.

46. Michno, *Handbook,* previously cited, p. 196. I disagree with Michno and would urge their avoidance, except perhaps in the revised United Methodist form mentioned earlier.

47. See, for example, Christopher Rowland, *Christian Origins* (London: SPCK, 1985), subtitled "An Account of the Setting and Character of the Most Important Messianic Sect in Judaism."

48. Marion Hatchett, *A Commentary on the American [Episcopal] Prayer Book* (New York: Seabury, 1981), p. 234.

49. Ruether, *Faith and Fratricide,* previously cited, p. 111.

50. Gager, *Origins,* previously cited, p. 152.

51. Ruether, *Faith and Fratricide,* previously cited, p. 68; see also Raymond Brown, *The Gospel according to John XIII-XXI* [The Anchor Bible] (Garden City, NY: Doubleday, 1970), p. 791ff., esp. pp. 792–793.

52. *A Liturgical Interpretation of Our Lord's Passion in Narrative Form* [Israel Study Group, Occasional Paper Number One](New York: The National Conference of Christians and Jews, 1977), pp. 1–2.

53. *Ibid.,* p. 2.

54. *Ibid.*

55. (New York: Paulist Press, 1982).

56. See, for example, "Paul and Torah" in *Anti-Semitism and the Foundations of Christianity,* ed. by Alan Davies (New York: Paulist Press, 1979).

57. Pp. 368–369.

58. *Christ in the Light of Christian-Jewish Dialogue,* previously cited, p. 137.

Chapter Two

Expansive Language
A Matter of Justice

Conversion is a curious business and certainly not all converts are alike. Some converts, for instance, remember the moment, the particulars, and some do not. I am in the second batch. I know only roughly

when this change of heart occurred. I know there was a time before and a time after—I can document it in my own writing—but as to exactly when and where I cannot say. What I am sure of is that the conversion was serious, thorough so far as I know, and enduring. I came to realize that words and what they declare or ignore are media of justice or its absence, health or harm, nurture or deprivation.

My conversion on the matter of language and justice, firstly with reference to the emancipation of women, was prepared by a prior awakening, one regarding the ordination of women to the presbyterate. Though I cannot put an exact date to this event either, I recall the circumstances vividly. I was the vicar of a pair of small congregations in the northeastern corner of Missouri, up the Mississippi from Hannibal. At the larger of the two, we had a regular Wednesday morning eucharist, typically (almost always) attended only by women. On one such Wednesday, in the company of five women, I stood reading Luke's gospel, chapter one beginning with verse 46. As I proclaimed these verses, the realization passed through me that these extraordinary words of Mary (and Hannah) were *not* words any woman was privileged to read in the eucharistic liturgy of the Episcopal Church. This was 1967 or '68. I was astounded and awakened amidst the Magnificat.

Although the particulars of my own conversion escape recollection and, hence, distinguish me from other more clear-minded converts, I share with these other converts the same commitment to the conversion enterprise. I begin this way in order to declare that I write as a convert, one persuaded that exclusivity can inhere in language, liturgical and otherwise, and that this exclusivity is a sin, particularly in liturgical language. Further, like some converts at least, I have lost my capacity to understand the perspective of the unconverted. That is, I have lost the ability to understand, or even tolerate, the arguments mounted by those who argue against inclusive/emancipatory/expansive language. And the logic of inclusivity in language is so persuasive, the necessity of justice so compelling as to render me useless in explaining how one could remain unconverted. This is especially true for me with regard to the women in my acquaintance for whom exclusive (and therefore by my terms "sinful") language is "no problem."

It is clear that a concern for just, expansive language has been a part of the process and products of liturgical revision in the Episcopal Church before now, before considering the "next" revision. The current revision of the Book of Common Prayer, within itself, testifies to the existence of this concern and to efforts to respond to it. One need only compare the texts in rites I and II to see the fruits of efforts on the parts of revisers to be more inclusive in our liturgical language. The same evidence is available, perhaps in greater abundance, in *The Hymnal 1982*. The pursuit of a more just vocabulary and form of expression is a matter with a history. What is needful now, as we look to a rebirth of the formal revision process, is a more thoroughgoing commitment to a more just liturgical vernacular.

Such a vernacular would be characterized by assumptions about uniformity and diversity that are distinguishable from those in the current revision. "Man" and its siblings would not be respected as generic terms for the human community and the experience of men would not survive as normative for the whole of humanity. With this norm as a first principle, the extension of its logic would be thoroughgoing.

The literature treating this subject matter is extensive and readily available. Most useful to my mind are three sources written by Episcopalians, interestingly enough, and one by a member of the Reformed Church. As an appendix to *The Supplemental Liturgical Materials,* published by the Standing Liturgical Commission in 1991, Leonel Mitchell offered a carefully reasoned and gently written discussion of the nature of liturgical language, the reasonableness of change in liturgical language and the premise for change in our time. He wrote, "To the extent that this traditional usage of English grammar causes worshipers to think of God as male or causes women to feel that their creation in God's image is being denied, it is a serious distortion of the meaning of what is being proclaimed."[1] This line is written with reference to the use of the male pronoun "he" in reference to God, but the same premise could well be cited for the use of generic male terms for all humanity.

The writings of Marjorie Procter-Smith have much to offer as conversion materials regarding the liberation of liturgical language. Two sources in particular are important. In her 1990 book, *In Her Own Rite: Constructing Feminist Liturgical Tradition,* Professor Procter-Smith, an Episcopalian teaching at Perkins School of Theology in Dallas, proposed a schema for a more just vernacular ranging from "nonsexist" to "inclusive" to "emancipatory."[2] She writes,

> Nonsexist language seeks to avoid gender-specific terms. Inclusive language seeks to balance gender references. Emancipatory language seeks to transform language use and to challenge stereotypical gender references.[3]

Observing that sexist or androcentric language "makes women invisible," she goes on to explain,

> Nonsexist language suggests that God does not regard our gender, or that our gender is not relevant to our relationship with God. In-

clusive language implies that God does regard our gender, but that both women and men possess equal status before God. Emancipatory language assumes that God is engaged in women's struggles for emancipation, even to the point of identifying with those who struggle . . . [E]mancipatory language must make women visible.[4]

It is surely a matter of justice for those who edit and create liturgical texts, including those who translate texts from earlier times and places, to "make women visible."

In her most recent book, *Praying with Our Eyes Open*, Prof. Procter-Smith contributes yet another potent observation. In her chapter entitled "Praying Between the Lines," she reports the experience of women who have found a way of praying "through" androcentric formulas by "praying between the lines." She speaks, further, of the necessity of simultaneous translation, rendering the androcentric text into a more generous, usable vernacular. "We grow accustomed . . . to translating as we go, reading ourselves into the text from which we have been excised, by reading behind the texts, reading the silences and the spaces, the absences and the omissions. We learn to hear words not spoken aloud, see signs unread by others. And we learn to keep our readings to ourselves."[5]

Here the author points to two matters of fragmentation, matters which justice ought to preclude. Firstly, there is the fragmentation of the gathered community created by the use of a vocabulary (and its underlying assumptions) which is not the *lingua franca* of that very community, a vocabulary which is not the natural, native tongue of the community. This fragmentation would not be tolerated if the community were recognized to be multi-lingual along ethnic or national lines.

The second fragmentation derives from the author's final comment, " . . . we learn to keep our readings to ourselves." Herein lie the seeds not only of fragmentation by also of isolation, the "reading" of the oppressed serving as the "code" among the isolated. Surely, no community, especially perhaps the community of the baptized, needs such isolation spawned and supported within itself by the language they use. Beyond this, of course, is the matter of the ownership and exercise of power, and the creation of continuous power contests between the "outside" patriarchal language and the "inside" translation and those who "understand" either.

The third writer to receive mention in this setting is Brian Wren, a minister of the Reformed Church in England, now writing and teaching in the United States. Among the books cited in this essay, his *What Language Shall I Borrow?* takes the unique perspective of being written self-consciously for a male readership. In a forthright and literate fashion, Dr. Wren displays and dissects "patriarchy" as a social and theological reality embedded in the way we (men and women) think and talk, and undertakes to find a language to serve as its replacement.[6]

From first reading, I have found this book persuasive in a most captivating fashion. For example, the author ends a section in which he explores males sexual violence by making this simple and profound observation, "We need a new, humane paradigm of manhood in which the 'true man' neither conquers nor protects, but simply behaves as a good neighbor to women, children, and other men"[7] In a later section, considering the life pattern of Jesus as a model for other males, Dr. Wren writes, "Jesus does not merely fail to uphold patriarchal norms or take a different direction. His whole ministry undermines those norms and gives us a vision of a different kind of society."[8] The realization of this vision is a task shared by women and men. These sources, either alone or in combination, along with countless others, provide powerful testimony to the necessities of justice in the reconstitution of our liturgical language. Those who are writing and will write new texts for the future revision of the Prayer Book are typically persuaded of this necessity and the emerging texts do and will show forth a deeper commitment to a vernacular that gathers up, one that requires no "translation" as Marjorie Procter-Smith speaks of it. The making more just of the older texts, the "received" texts as it were, remains the problem it was in revising the current edition of the Prayer Book and in the making of the current Hymnal, though now the use of biblical texts taken from the NRSV will be a boon.

The real struggle in this regard will likely be the matter of the retention of the Rite I formulas, unrelieved of their patriarchal burden. In this case, however, it is not simply a matter of "fixing" the language but also of re-engaging the imagery as well. Though Rite II needs similar re-engagement, Rite I needs it more and more fundamentally. It may be helpful here to recall the convictions about vernacular liturgy held by Thomas Cranmer, the "author" of the first two Books of Common Prayer (1549 and 1552). It was Cranmer's conviction that putting the liturgy in the vernacular was absolutely necessary in order (1) to achieve a higher level of participation among the faithful and (2) to achieve in the Body of Christ a fuller degree of edification.[9] These two necessities, participation and edification, remain central to liturgical revision, as much today as in the 1540's. And for Cranmer as for ourselves, expressing the liturgy in the vernacular is a matter of justice.

What may prove to be ironic here is that by retaining Thomas Cranmer's convictions about vernacular liturgy, we may find a warrant for letting go of some (at least) of Cranmer's language. In any case, it remains true that the crafting of new texts using a more just vernacular will come more easily than the renovation of older ones.[10]

One needs to remember, in all this, that the language of the liturgy is only partially contained in the texts provided in the Prayer Book. There is a much broader context in which these words serve. The words of the formal texts are joined by other words, those from the Bible, those used to do the congregation's business by way of announcements, those words offered in song, those words employed in the fashioning of indigenous prayers and those used in preaching. Whatever matters of justice are rightly raised about the formal texts, these same matters of justice must also inform these other words. The church's commitment to justice, when it is shown forth in texts, must find worthy companions in the rest of the language of the liturgy. All our speaking must speak justly.

Extending the context further, we need to recognize that the non-verbal dimension of the liturgical event constitutes a kind of "language," too. Clearly, the critique to which we have pointed and which we have recapitulated in some small measure has most often been aimed at words (and the assumptions that support them). But this critique ought also to call us to be mindful of non-verbal, spatial and gestural justice as well.

When we think of any liturgical event, the Sunday Holy Eucharist for example, what we experience is only partially represented by the Prayer Book texts and rubrics. Much of the experience is unknown to the texts beyond the rubrical directions. The liturgical space, vesture, furnishings, liturgical objects, gestures and personnel and their actions—this level of the liturgical experience is not "controlled" by the text. If we are to use "expansive" eyes and hearts to assess the texts, such must also be used to determine the justice done and seen to be done in the liturgy as a totality. Do the postures and gestures declare and foster just relationships? Does the liturgical space evince hospitality and invite a just level of participation by all? Pursuit of these questions and others like them ought to describe and direct our thinking about "revision." And if we were to come to some common and clear view as to what makes for justice in these matters, who is to advocate it, teach it, model it such that the church at large will see and know?

In the end, it seems to me, the real issue is the matter of power, or better perhaps, the twin issues of authority and consent. By whose authority might this more just vernacular be employed and whose consent or pleasure must be sought in the undertaking?

Writing in his fifteen-year-old and yet still challenging book, *The Integrity of Anglicanism*, Stephen Sykes suggested that those who revise the texts and fashion the rubrics in the Prayer Book occupy the real center of authority within Anglicanism. Sykes put it this way, " . . . the decision-making process whereby liturgies are changed . . . is the basic seat of authority in the Anglican Church, and the basic exercise of that authority is the power to enforce the liturgy."[11] Whatever the truth of this assertion, it is tested every Sunday as texts and rubrics are routinely abridged, reinterpreted or ignored. In any particular place, whatever is customary, "traditional" as it were, is going to contain and exercise the real power, authority and consent, rubrical direction or no, General Convention or no. But the broader issue is the question of justice itself. The texts and rubrics in the Book of Common Prayer, if they are to promote justice, must also mirror justice. I am persuaded, as many others are, that the ritual life of a community is formative of the heart of that community as well as being expressive of the convictions and story of that community. This being so, the liturgy, while intending the formation of a more just community, must also be expressive of that community's intention to do justice. "Fixing the words" is not the point; justice, and godly mercy, are. Here we are at the essential matter. Are we (that is the church, not just liturgical revisers) able or willing to see the need for a revised liturgical vernacular as a matter of justice at all? Is the dream of a common language sufficiently alluring to elicit from us all a commitment to revision for justice's sake? If we commit ourselves to justice and say "yes" to these questions, we will surely have a wide array of possibilities available to us and a more vivid, hopeful future. A negative answer will bring only loss and despair. The choice is up to us.[12]

---

1. (New York: Church Hymnal), p. 63. This same essay appeared in the earlier publication of some of these "materials" when they appeared as "texts." I once spoke at a meeting of General Convention delegates from the Dioceses of Dallas and Fort Worth. My task was to discuss with them the rationale and substance of the proposed supplemental ("inclusive language") texts. My intent was to commend Prof. Mitchell's essay to them as a clearly written and moderate presentation on the matter. As I listened to the speaker who preceded me, who spoke vigorously against even the idea of the texts, I heard Prof. Mitchell's insightful essay condemned and ridiculed. When it came my turn to speak, I took the floor, so to speak, with that introduction. As one person said to me afterwards, "The floor was not level." Indeed!

2. (Nashville: Abingdon), p. 63ff.

3. *Ibid.*

4. *Ibid.*, pp. 66–67.

5. (Nashville: Abingdon, 1995), p. 32. Prof. Procter-Smith is relying on Elizabeth Castelli in this instance.

6. (New York: Crossroad, 1993).

7. *Ibid.*, p. 43.

8. *Ibid.*, p. 179.

9. These convictions were expressed in his Preface to the first Book of Common Prayer (1549).

10. I am reminded of an article written years ago by the late Erik Routley, hymnwriter and composer, in which he struggled with the matter of revising hymns in terms of what we are calling "justice." He set out an array of alternatives, including setting a hymn aside if it could not be "redeemed." See "Sexist Language: A View from a Distance," in *Worship* 53/1 (January, 1979), pp. 2–11.

11. (London: Mowbrays, 1979 [1978]), p. 96.

12. It would be important to recognize that even by shifting the assumptions about liturgical revision to "expansive" assumptions, there are still significant debates and disagreements to engage and resolve. As one would rightly expect, a common language remains yet a "dream" even among those committed to its achievement. Central to this is the matter of the way that older assumptions can be used to test newer ones, while allowing the newer ones to discipline the older ones. How this kind of reciprocity or complementarity among and between assumptions is to serve the church remains for us to explore.

Chapter Three

The Prayer Book
Theology of Ministry

The Book of Common Prayer

The theology of ministry contained in or taught by the Book of Common Prayer is a complex, "emergent" theology. That it is "emergent" will be clearer when the next revision is produced, as that revision likely

will evince a more clear and unified expression of the strands of theology which are currently entangled in the Prayer Book 1979. The entanglement is due to the fact that at the time of publication, the church's thinking on ministry was undergoing reformulation, moving from a view which would understand "ministry" to mean "ordained ministry" to a view which would treat "ministry" as a much broader idea, one inclusive of the whole church.

What one finds, therefore, in the Prayer Book is these two ideas at work, sometimes compatibly and sometimes not. The presence of these two ideas makes impossible the task of describing and exploring the Prayer Book's theology of ministry as if it were a unified theology. Therefore, for the purposes of this essay, we shall be concerned to present the newer, "emergent" theology, making reference to the older view, principally in section 6, wherein some critique will be offered of the entanglement mentioned above. Readers wishing to pursue "ministry" understood to mean "ordained ministry" are referred to the essays in the collection treating "ordination" and the "orders" of ministry.[1]

The "emergent" theology of ministry presented by the Prayer Book can be gotten at in two different fashions. The most direct method is to inquire of the Catechism. The less direct is to explore the way the Prayer Book talks about ministers and ministry in both texts and rubrics.

The Catechism answers the question "Who are the ministers of the Church?" by saying, "The ministers of the Church are lay persons, bishops, priests, and deacons" (BCP, 855). This way of both putting and answering the question moves considerably beyond the catechetical view expressed in previous editions of the Prayer Book. For example, in the 1928 revision, in the second Office of Instruction, the question was asked rather differently. There it said, "What orders of Ministers are there in the Church?" To this query the prescribed reply was, "Bishops, Priests, and Deacons; which orders have been in the Church from the earliest times" (BCP, 294).

The difference between the questions and their formal answers testifies to the intent of the 1979 Prayer Book on this important doctrinal question and illustrates an important instance in the development of doctrine. The catechetical evidence is clear that the current revision intends to teach the church that a proper understanding of ministry must be inclusive of all the baptized, and is not limited to some smaller portion of the church.

The Catechism goes on to illuminate the character of the several ministries of the church. Of greatest moment for our considerations here is the answer to the question, "What is the ministry of the laity?" The answer given is, "The ministry of lay persons is to represent Christ and his Church; to bear witness to him wherever they may be; and, according to the gifts given them, to carry on Christ's work of reconciliation in the world; and to take their place in the life, worship, and governance of the Church" (BCP, 855). This question and answer are followed by similar questions and appropriate answers regarding bishops, priests and deacons.

What is notable here is the Prayer Book's catechetical effort to offer a theology in which mutuality, balance and proportion rather than clerical exclusivity characterize the church's teaching. Differentiation without dominance is an aspect. This definition of "ministry" is not built upon hierarchical distinctions between laity and clergy but is rather inclusive and integrative of both. In this way, this definition tends to suggest that such distinctions as lay/clergy are inappropriate, *at the level of definition.*

In addition to studying the Catechism, there is yet a second method by which to inquire into the Prayer Book's teaching on ministry. This is to examine the textual and rubrical evidence. One needs to be careful here, however. Liturgical leadership in the tradition of the Episcopal Church is a particular responsibility of priests and bishops and the texts enshrined in the Prayer Book obviously evince this fact. Yet, because the liturgical necessity for priestly ministry is specific and limited, the texts and rubrics, for the most part, can give added testimony to the mutuality and distributive character of ministry to which the Catechism points so clearly.

In the Daily Office, the liturgical leader is called the "Officiant" and the supposition is that that person is one of the baptized. Ordination is not a prerequisite. Provision is made for the work of an ordained person but that work is not essential to the Office. Similarly, throughout the eucharistic texts, the word "Minister" is used to indicate portions of the liturgy for which ordination is not appropriate or necessary. In fact, the rubrical information that precedes both Rites I and II (322/354) makes clear the appropriateness (some might say the necessity) of the distribution of roles and ministries among the gathered community, laypersons, deacons, priests and bishops each having their rightful place in the ordering of things.

One also sees in virtually every liturgical form a dialogical format which, in and of itself, suggests the mutuality of ministry which is to characterize the church's self-understanding. Dialogue, litany, call and response, ordered distribution of roles and work—all of these illustrate (or can be seen to illustrate) the view put directly in the Catechism. The texts and rubrics intend to present an integrated view toward the understanding of the ministry of the church.

Most conclusively, one needs to look at a particular moment in the liturgy for Holy Baptism. After the candidates have received the sacramental action of water, signing (perhaps oil) and prayer, the body of the faithful welcome the newly initiated by saying, "We receive you into the household of God. Confess the faith of Christ crucified, proclaim his resurrection, and share with us in his eternal priesthood" (BCP, 308). In a capsule as clear as the Catechism but more evocative of action and responsibility, the Prayer Book attests to the incorporation of all the baptized into the ministry of Jesus. It is most particularly here that the Prayer Book's theology of ministry is to be seen. "Ministry" is the expression and consequence of baptism.

Holy Scriptures

The biblical moorings for the Prayer Book's "emergent" theology of ministry are found primarily in the Gospels and the letters of Paul. It is most clearly rooted in Jesus' discussion of leadership in the community of his followers, in the setting out of his own life as the content of ministry for his followers, in the body metaphor used by Paul in I Corinthians and in his conclusion to Galatians 3. To this list we will add a particularly apt (but problematic) citation from 1 Peter.

At the heart of the biblical understanding of the developing Christian church is the idea of community, an interdependent and mutually attentive gathering among which the gifts of its members determined the role or work assigned or expected. The style in which these gifts were to be exercised was presented by Jesus to his closest companions.

In Matthew 20:20ff. (Cf. Mk 10:35–45, Lk 22:24–27), Jesus is asked to accord places of privilege to James and John. This request prompts him to speak directly to the manner in which leadership is to be exercised among his followers. Scorning the style most readily associated with "the Gentiles," Jesus says "it shall not be so among you." Instead of those who "lord it over them," his followers were to pattern their lives after his own example, wherein they see servanthood as the chief characteristic. " . . . [W]hoever would be great among you must be your servant, and whoever would be first among you must be your slave; even as the Son of Man came not to be served but to serve . . . " (Mt. 20:26b-28a)[2]

This emphasis in the teachings of Jesus combines readily with what Paul says about the life of the Christian community in his first letter to Corinth. Chapter 12 is concerned with the distribution and interplay of gifts, about which Paul did not want his readers to be "uninformed." His persistent theme in this discussion is the unity of the community, the unity of baptism and the unity of the Spirit into which all were gathered by the baptismal waters. "For just as the body is one and has many members, and all the members of the body, though many, are one body, so it is with Christ . . . For the body does not consist of one member but of many" (I Cor 12:12,14).

The mutuality and interdependence implicit in the body metaphor is extended later in the same chapter. He writes, "If one member suffers, all suffer together; if one member is honored, all rejoice together" (I Cor 12:26). By this reading, each member participates in the others' existence fully, without duplication or competition. Paul's point is that as this mutuality and reciprocity are characteristic of the human body, so it must also be characteristic of the followers of Jesus Christ.[3]

Further, in Paul's letter to the Galatians, he discusses the consequences of "putting on Christ," that is, baptism. "For as many of you as were baptized into Christ have put on Christ." By this action, "there is neither Jew nor Greek, there is neither slave nor free, there is neither male nor female; for you are all one in Christ Jesus" (Gal 3:27–28). Here Paul describes most clearly the unity of the baptismal community. And the power of his hyperbole makes the most powerful point. The distinctions within the community are gathered into a more potent unity. The categories of separation are made pale by the waters of baptism.

Edward Schillebeeckx, writing in *The Church with a Human Face*, and commenting on this Galatians passage, locates the genesis of Paul's description in "a pre-Pauline tradition" in which one sees quite readily what the author calls "early-Christian egalitarian ecclesiology." Schillebeeckx points out, however, that such an ecclesiology does not, as the body imagery discussed earlier also does not, exclude leadership and authority.[4]

For the work and responsibilities which flow out of "putting on Christ," we must return to the Gospels. The ministry to which all the baptized are called is the ministry of Jesus. This ministry is not the special preserve of certain persons but the calling of all the baptized. The content of this ministry is best articulated in the judgment speech recorded in Matthew 25 and in the "great commission" in Matthew 28.

In Matthew 25:34ff., Jesus makes plain the standard of authenticity in ministry, on the basis of which one is either "sheep" or "goats." To all his hearers, he declares that feeding the hungry, quenching the thirst of the thirsty, welcoming the stranger, clothing the naked and visiting those in prison are the hallmark of his expectations. Doing this work is Jesus' common expectation of all his followers, hence, the work of ministry for the whole church.

Matthew ends his gospel with Jesus commissioning his followers to do the work of evangelization, again a task held in common by the followers of Jesus. "Go, therefore, and make disciples . . ." (Mt 28:19) This charge underlies the latter petitions in the Baptismal Covenant (BCP, 305) and gives explicit direction to the energies of the church. It again is inclusive of all the followers of Jesus.

In conclusion, it is appropriate to notice 1 Peter 2:9 since it provides language that will reappear in the tradition and which forms part of the Prayer Book's vocabulary. "You are a chosen race, a royal priesthood, a holy nation, God's own people, in order that you may proclaim the mighty acts of him who called you out of darkness into his marvelous light." This text is clearly supportive of claims about the breadth of the ministry within the community of the baptized. The language of priesthood, although it is used in the New Testament only with reference to

Jesus and to the community of the baptized, is historically associated with the ordained ministry and is so treated in the tradition until challenged by the reformers. This fact makes difficult the retrieval of "priestly" language with reference to the whole church.

Historical Evidences

Exploring the historical evidences poses a significant problem at the outset. The problem is presented by the word "ministry" itself. As it is typically translated from other languages and as it is treated in source material, the word is most commonly understood as what we here would call "ordained ministry," a distinction not always clearly made even in the Prayer Book, as we will discuss later. Consequently, one must search for and select sources which approach the issue treated in this essay in a particular and appropriate fashion. "Ministry," as a blanket term, without being nuanced by what we have said earlier, simply will not serve as an entry into research.[5]

Further, as we have tried to make clear in the selection of biblical evidences, the theology of "ministry" we are exploring (and which we find "emergent" in the Prayer Book) is *not* one dependent on social hierarchy. (It is, however, like the "body" to which Paul refers, expressive of organization and order.) Consequently, given the fact that much of what history provides about "ministry" (meaning "ordained ministry") is typically accompanied by convictions about the necessity of social hierarchy, one must be all the more specific and careful in choosing sources.

Alexandre Faivre, writing in his *The Emergence of the Laity in the Early Church*, makes clear that for the first two centuries of the church's life, there were no categories in the life of the church which functioned then as "clergy/lay" have subsequently and seem to in the present. The *kleros*, the lot or inheritance, was that of the whole community of the baptized and not simply some segment of it. Faivre's research suggests that what justified this sense of being a part of the *kleros* was "neither a function of government or direction, nor a more advanced level of holiness or any special merit, but membership of the people."[6]

Further, the author says that during the first two centuries of the church's life, "there is no theological argument [offered] justifying a dichotomy between the ministers of the altar and the people. The question of the laity is only introduced if we create an artificial anachronism."[7] It is also true to say, however, that by the beginning of the third century, "the need for the people of God to be split into two groups—clergy and faithful believers—is postulated in all ecclesiological teaching."[8]

Any challenge to this subdivision of the *kleros* in subsequent centuries typically took the form of anti-clericalism, rather than a positive effort to restore a unified understanding of the church's call to service. In truth, the recovery of a more whole and integrated view of the nature of the church and its ministry would await the revival of baptismal theology which has expressed itself (and is expressing itself) in the current moment.

One legacy of the distinction between clergy and laity was the recurrent theological habit of defining the church with specific or exclusive reference to the ordained, particularly the bishop, to the exclusion of the rest of the baptized. This traditional approach was challenged from time to time, none more pointedly than that offered by the 14th-century political theorist, Marsiglio of Padua, whose *Defensor Pacis* was published in 1324.

A treatise on political philosophy, this text served the reformation era as a treasury of ideas. Though certainly if asked, Marsiglio would have understood "ministry" to mean "ordained ministry," his definition of the church is fundamental to the views of later generations. In his second discourse, in contrast to definitions of the church which fix on the clergy, Marsiglio writes, "the 'church' means the whole body of the faithful who believe in and invoke the name of Christ, and all the parts of this whole body in any community, even the household." He goes on to say that this was "the sense in which ['the church'] was customarily used among the apostles and the primitive church."[9] The inclusiveness of this definition is instrumental to any claims about the interrelationship of clergy and laity in the work and ministry of the church.

With Martin Luther we find a complex of ideas relevant to our concerns and the recovery of a central biblical image around which Luther would build his argument. In his diatribe, "The Babylonian Captivity of the Church," Luther argues against the exclusivist claims made by Rome as to the nature of priesthood. "Now we," he writes, "who have been baptized, are all uniformly priests by virtue of that very fact. The only addition received by the priests is the office of preaching, and even this with our Consent . . . Thus it says in I Peter 2[:9], 'Ye are an elect race, a royal priesthood, and a priestly kingdom.' It follows that all of us who are Christians are also priests." [10] Several pages later, he says, "every one who knows that he is a Christian should be fully assured that all of us alike are priests, and that we all have the same authority in regard to the word and the sacraments, although no one has the right to administer them without the consent of the members of his church, or by the call of the majority." [11] Further, in his "Open Letter to the Christian Nobility," also dated 1520, Luther asserted, "those now called 'religious,' i.e., priests, bishops, and popes, possess no further or greater dignity than other Christians, except that their duty is to expound the word of God and sacraments—that being their office." [12]

With Luther, then, we get a clear articulation of the common source out of which all Christian ministry grows. That common source is baptism. We also get into rather murky territory with the language of "priesthood," a term explored elsewhere in this volume. [13] For our purposes, what is important is to see a view of the church and the calling to ministry which is integrative of all the baptized, clearly a forebear of the "emergent" view in the Prayer Book. [14]

The Anglican Tradition

For Anglicans, the strand of Prayer Book theology we are chasing is a modern discovery, however sympathetic some earlier Anglicans might have been to the ideas of Luther. [15] Searches through the Thirty-Nine Articles, Hooker, the Caroline Divines, Charles Simeon and the Tractarians frequently bring one into conversations about ministry, yet this is typically in reference to "ordained" ministry and associated with a structured view of society that is not a part of the theology of the current Prayer Book.

At the same time, in a certain respect, one might claim support from Hooker but only with a good deal of care. When Hooker speaks of the relationship of clergy and lay people, what Paul Avis has called "a balance and coherence of clergy and laity," what is actually at hand is discussion of the relationship between ecclesial authority and civil authority, and the coincidence of church and commonwealth.[16] This is a rather different matter than that contained in the current revision of the Prayer Book.

In this century, however, ample sources are available to suggest some lineage for the current revision. In the literature generated from the Lambeth Conferences, there is a clear consciousness of the interrelatedness of all Christian ministry. In the "Encyclical Letter to the Faithful in Jesus Christ" from the Bishops at Lambeth, 1958, the following observation was made, "There is a growing recognition today that too sharp a distinction has been made between clergy and laity. All baptized persons have the priestly vocation of offering life as a living sacrifice, acceptable to God through Jesus Christ. There is a ministry for every member of Christ . . ."[17] Making reference to this passage in "Laymen in Mission," an essay in the collection *Lambeth Essays on Ministry,* edited by the Archbishop of Canterbury, Douglas Webster points out that "In the past the assumption has too often been that the clergy are those who minister and the laity are those who are ministered to. But in the New Testament ministry is understood primarily in terms of function rather than status. All Christians belong to the one people of God, all have some ministry to perform in the Body of Christ, and all have some share in the total mission of the Church in the world."[18] He goes on to say, however, that "Ministry is not to be confused with *the* ministry, that is the *ordained* ministry."[19] In so saying, the mutuality of ministry is intersected.

Similarly, it is common to the Lambeth documents, while speaking of ministry as appropriate to the church as a whole, to discuss "the ministry," meaning explicitly clergy. This is essentially the predicament of the Prayer Book in its current revision.

A formal and more or less "official" view on the question of ministry is contained in *The Blue Book* of the General Convention of the Episcopal Church, 1988. In a statement called "Theology of Ministry" contained in the report of the Council for the Development of Ministry (meaning, ironically, "ordained ministry") one reads as follows, "Ministry is total because it belongs to each baptized person. No one is superior; no one is exempt . . . The Church is given by God to serve the community of the baptized in its gathered state and to move them out into the world to love and serve the Lord there as pastors, as evangelists, as teachers, and as witnesses. Baptism is the root of total ministry; the community of the baptized forms total ministry; the world is the stage for total ministry." [20] This expansive statement recounts and reflects the implications of at least part of the Prayer Book's teachings.

In 1977, James C. Fenhagen published *Mutual Ministry.*[21] In this small book, the author presented the view of ministry which we are calling the "emergent" view contained in the Prayer Book. Central to Fenhagen's view is the following statement: "The ministry of the church is always the ministry of the *laos*. It is the mutual ministry of clergy and laity alike, each supporting and challenging the other in the unique functions they are called upon to perform." [22] When Fenhagen includes the clergy in the *laos*, he moves in the direction to which Alexandre Faivre pointed in a citation above, when he demonstrated that in earlier times, the *kleros* ("lot") was understood to be the circumstance of the whole church and not some smaller segment of it.

Writing from the point of view of the contemporary Church of England, Robin Greenwood proposes a "collaborative ministry" among all the baptized, rooted theologically in a social view of the Trinity.[23] "The being of the Church should echo the dynamic relations between the three Persons who together constitute the triune God." [24] Here Greenwood testifies, as Fenhagen does, to the interplay of order without hierarchy and mutuality in this vision of ministry and church.

Finally, Tim Bradshaw, writing in *The Olive Branch: An Evangelical Anglican Doctrine of the Church,* asserts, "The ministry, the service, of Christ in the whole church means that the whole body is called to play its part; the ordained ministry subserves the ministry of all the people . . . Rather than being a focus of the church's ministry, [ordained ministry] is the office to promote and release a wealth of ministries, all seeking to conform to the mind of Christ as known in the word."[25] This view is quite congruent with what we find in one clear strand of teaching in the current revision of the Prayer Book.

Contemporary Ecumenical Theology

In his book, *Diakonia: Re-interpreting the Ancient Sources,* John N. Collins reviews a wide variety of ecumenical sources which speak of our theme. Among denominational sources—Roman Catholic, Anglican, Lutheran or Reformed—there is a clear common-mindedness expressed at one level. To cite but one example, a World Council of Churches document, dated 1963, asserts that "ministry is the responsibility of the whole body and not only of those who are ordained," and that "Christ calls the whole Church into his whole ministry."[26] Similar citations can be offered from more recent WCC sources, e.g., the Lima Document, in which one reads, "The word *ministry* in its broadest sense denotes the service to which the whole people of God is called, whether as individuals, as a local community, or as the Universal Church."[27]

In addition to such common-mindedness, however, there is another current. This second current is suggested, for example, in the ARCIC document, *The Final Report.* While asserting that "ordained ministry can only be rightly understood within [a] broader context of various ministries,"[28] this same ordained ministry, when properly viewed, is "not an extension of the common Christian priesthood but belongs to another realm of the gifts of the Spirit."[29] This view attests to the unresolvedness of the tension between assertions as to the universality of baptismal ministry and the separate uniqueness of ordained ministry. As we have indicated earlier, this same tension resides in the current revision of the Book of Common Prayer.

Personal Critique

The theology of ministry which we have described as "emergent" or "nascent" in the 1979 Prayer Book points a direction towards which subsequent revisions must continue to move, if this understanding of ministry is the mind of the church. In continuing in this direction, important matters will need consideration. Principal among these is the coherence of the doctrines in the Prayer Book that express most directly teachings on ministry, and the gaining of consistency in the vocabulary used throughout the rubrics and instructions.

If the view towards ministry which we have described is to find fuller expression, then the relationship between the ordination rites and the rites of Christian initiation will need to be considered *together*.[30] The question will be, "How can an *integrated* theology of ministry be taught by the Prayer Book which is consistent throughout the several rites?"

The challenge in this regard will be reconciling the received tradition as regards ordination rites, a tradition which perpetuates the suggestion that "ministry" and "ordained ministry" are interchangeable terms, and the awakening conviction that ministry, rightly so-called, belongs no more to ordained people than to the rest of the baptized. Putting baptismal rites and ordination rites together will cause us to reconsider language like "ordination to the sacred priesthood" (BCP, 527) and "ordination to the sacred order of deacons" (BCP, 537), and require that we examine the ritual patterns of baptism and ordination so as to make them congruent with the theological substance we intend to express. (This same concern will need to be brought to a review of the "Celebration of a New Ministry."[31])

Secondly, if we intend that the Prayer Book teach a theology of ministry that is rooted in the fact that one is *baptized* for ministry and that among the baptized, some are ordained to particular callings, then we will need to reform our rubrical and instructional vocabulary. For example, at the time appointed for the exchange of the peace in both rites I and II, following the congregational exchange between the presider and the assembly, the rubric reads, "Then the Ministers and People may greet one another in the name of the Lord" (BCP, 332, 360). If "ministry" is an inclusive category gathering the baptized, then how is this instruction to be understood? It is obviously clarified and made theologically consistent if changed to read "Then the liturgical ministers and people . . ."

Further, among the prayers gathered under the heading "For the Ministry" in the section of collects for various occasions, of the three collects offered, two clearly relate to the "ordained" ministry, one of which speaks of choosing "fit persons for the ministry" (BCP, 205). This way of speaking is rooted in assumptions obviously still loose in the current revision of the Prayer Book but which will need to be reconsidered if a consistent and integrative theology of ministry is to be taught and enacted by the church.

The preface to the ordinal (BCP, 510) exhibits care on this point which should characterize the rest of the Prayer Book, at least to a degree. The preface is consistent in speaking about "ordained" ministries throughout, rather than to suggest that ordination is to "ministry" more generally understood. At the same time, the preface concludes with language that we have suggested will need to be reviewed if consistency is to be achieved. The final line of the preface ends by referring to "the sacred orders of bishops, priests and deacons."

Other similar examples could be cited but they would all point in the same direction, namely, toward the need for a careful and committed review of the texts available, testing them as to their congruence with the conviction that the ministry of the church is shared among the baptized and is not the exclusive or even particular work or calling of only some few. The results of such a test, however, should not suggest that the church is without the need of focussed expressions of this ministry. The theology of ministry aborning in the Prayer Book is not innocent of the need for order nor disregarding of the particular callings of deacons, presbyters and bishops. It is, however, such as to require reformation of our vocabulary and thereby a reformation of what we teach.[32]

What is at hand in this theology of ministry is a kind of balance and mutuality which is difficult to find in current practice but which one can imagine with eagerness. T.S. Eliot, writing in "Little Gidding" gives us a picture of the kind of interconnectedness and reciprocity that this theology of ministry contains. In pursuit of the "phrase or sentence that is right," Eliot holds up this possibility, put parenthetically, "(where every word is at home,/ Taking its place to support the others,/ The word neither diffident nor ostentatious,/ An easy commerce of the old and the new,/ The common word exact without vulgarity,/ The formal word precise but not pedantic,/ The complete consort dancing together) . . ."[33]

This notion of ministry as a "complete consort dancing together" is often challenged in the real life of the church, a challenge consequent upon the failure of clergy and the rest of the baptized to see clearly its merits and their collaborative failure to carry it out. At the same time, there are those like John Snow who wonder whether such a view is appropriate from the outset. Writing in *A Vocation to Risk,* Snow suggests that the pitfalls attached to "mutual ministry" outweigh its benefits, when tested against the best examples of the older, hierarchical model. The fact that history is filled with examples of hierarchical church structures, Snow suggests, is because such structures "tend to be stable and enduring; they often cultivate a profound sense of belonging and a sense of safety."[34] These same characteristics do not surface, in the author's view, in more "non-hierarchical, egalitarian and participatory institutions."[35]

Prof. Snow's discussion illustrates, in its way, the dilemma inherent in the Prayer Book's "emergent" theology of ministry. The views expressed in the Prayer Book represent two strands, one committed to order and rooted in ordination and hierarchy, the other committed to order and rooted in baptism and mutuality. The church's experience with the former far exceeds that with the latter, and preference for the former may have as much to do with the preponderance and dominance of male clergy as with any other single factor.

Pastoral Application

The theology of ministry expressive of the conviction that baptism is the foundation for ministry will integrate and discipline all of the ways such ministry comes to flower. In particular, it will change what we teach about the nature of ministry and the church, and it will change the way we understand the particular work and calling of ordained people. Here we would be well advised to regard the calling to ordination as a calling primarily to liturgical work, following the line taken by Gordon Lathrop in *Holy Things: A Liturgical Theology.*[36] Lathrop writes, "Those who have the ministry of presiding will be continually invited to take joy in their circumscribed and yet immensely important tasks. They are to preside at baptisms, to preach Christ from the scriptures that have been read, to give thanks at table, to see to it that a collection for the poor is taken, and to reconcile the estranged to the purposes of the meeting. That is all they are to do under charge from their ritual appointment."[37] Lathrop articulates essentially what the current ordination rite says about the work of the presbyter and in so doing, confronts the fact that priests are often asked to do things for which *training* is necessary but for which *ordination* is not.

A more modest conviction about the nature of ordained ministry would testify to the fact that "ministry" is a larger idea than "ordained ministry" and would require a fundamental rethinking of preparation for ordination as well as the nature of the ministry acted out by most parishes and missions.

---

1. This is a reference to other chapters in the book to which this essay was a contribution. At the time of the publication of *Moving the Furniture, Prayer Book Doctrine* remains as yet unpublished. It is forthcoming from Church Publishing.

2. One might combine with Jesus' emphasis that of Paul in Ephesians 5:21, "Be subject to one another out of reverence for Christ." At the same time, one would want to be careful about the application of the verses immediately following, ones which treat being "subject" to one another. [All biblical citations are taken from the New Revised Standard Version.]

3. See the discussion on this text in Wayne A. Meeks, *The First Urban Christians: The Social World of the Apostle Paul* (New York: Yale University Press, 1983), pp. 89–90.

4. (New York: Crossroad, 1985), p. 39.

5. Very early in the church's life, "ministry" came to mean "ordained ministry." "Although the Sacrament of Holy Baptism consecrates every Christian to a life of ministry, from earliest time the community of the baptized has set apart some individuals to function as leaders of the communities of faith." Carl A. Volz, *Pastoral Life and Practice in the Early Church* (Minneapolis: Augsburg, 1990), p. 9. Historical sources tend to treat only those "set apart" as "ministers."

6. (New York: Paulist, 1990), p. 6.

7. *Ibid.*, p. 210.

8. *Ibid.*, p. 212.

9. Translated with an introduction by Alan Gewirth (New York: Harper and Row, 1956), Discourse II, Chapter II, p. 103.

10. *Martin Luther: Selections from His Writings,* edited and with an Introduction by John Dillenberger (Garden City, NY: Anchor Books, 1961), p. 345.

11. *Ibid.*, p. 349.

12. *Ibid.*, pp. 409–410.

13. "Elsewhere" in this sentence means elsewhere in *Prayer Book Doctrine.* On another matter, the "murkiness" of the "priesthood" part of the priesthood of all believers is amply demonstrated as one peruses Cyril Eastwood's two volume *The Royal Priesthood of the Faithful* (Minneapolis: Augsburg, 1963) and *The Priesthood of All Believers* (London: The Epworth Press, 1960).

14. Throughout this historical section, and the section to follow, one is tantalized with the thought that an exploration of the history of "confirmation" might yield a continuous thread of theory that would, in turn, contribute positively to our explorations regarding "ministry." See, for example, Gerard Austin, *The Rite of Confirmation: Anointing with the Spirit* (New York: Pueblo, 1985) and *Made, Not Born* [no editor] (Notre Dame, IN: University of Notre Dame Press for the Murphy Center for Liturgical Research, 1976).

15. See, for example, Paul Avis, *Anglicanism and the Christian Church* (Minneapolis: Fortress, 1989), *passim.*

16. See Avis, *Ibid.*

17. Lambeth 1958, 1.26.

18. (London: SPCK, 1968/1969), p. 1.

19. *Ibid.*

20. *The Blue Book: Reports of the Committees, Commissions, Boards and Agencies of the General Convention of the Episcopal Church* (Detroit, MI, July, 1988), p. 234.

21. (New York: Seabury Press).

22. *Ibid.*, pp. 29–30.

23. *Transforming Priesthood* (London: SPCK, 1994), p. 48.

24. *Ibid.*, p. 109.

25. (Carlisle, UK: Paternoster Press, 1992), pp. 158–159.

26. (New York: Oxford University Press, 1990), p. 28.

27. *Baptism, Eucharist and Ministry* [WCC Faith and Order Paper No. 111](Geneva: World Council of Churches, 1982), p. 21.

28. Anglican-Roman Catholic International Commission (Cincinnati, OH: Forward Movement, 1982), p. 30.

29. *Ibid.*, p. 36.

30. See the essay, "De-coding the Obvious: Reflections on Baptismal Ministry in the Episcopal Church," elsewhere in the current volume.

31. Stephen M. Kelsey has begun such a review in "Celebrating Baptismal Ministry at the Welcoming of New Ministers" in *Baptism and Ministry: Liturgical Studies One,* edited by Ruth A. Meyers (New York: Church Hymnal, 1994).

32. This "reformation" in our teaching would also include abandoning ordination language as regards Christian initiation. This language is exemplified by A. Theodore Eastman in his otherwise excellent book, *The Baptizing Community.* Eastman says, *"Baptism is ordination to the principal order of ministry."* This kind of language will need repair in the future, if baptism is to be taken to be the avenue to ministry. (New York: Seabury, 1982), p. 35.

33. "Little Gidding," V, *The Complete Poems and Plays, 1909–1950* (New York: Harcourt, Brace and World, 1971), p. 144.

34. (Cambridge, MA: Cowley, 1992), p. 105.

35. *Ibid.*, p. 106.

36. (Minneapolis: Fortress, 1993).

37. *Ibid.*, p. 201.

Part Two

Doing
Something
Different

Chapter Four

The Eucharistic Assembly
Who Presides?

"Who presides?" It is not a common or predictable question for Anglicans. The matter of presiding at the church's eucharistic assembly is virtually a forgone conclusion—a question not asked. Hence, no decision is really made. The answer is given—the priest presides. Yet, both imagination and recent history suggest that even for Anglicans, if given

the opportunity, the question will surface in a variety of fairly ordinary situations. And, indeed, for some it arises naturally in the course of ecumenical conversation and, consequently, insinuates itself into Anglican consciousness. Asking the question, then, carries with it the assumption that something other than the "standard" answer might be forthcoming.

In this brief essay, we propose to explore this question—"who presides?"—in the following manner. Firstly, we will consider the circumstances in which the question might or does arise. Having described these with some care, we will explore two alternative answers. Our intention in this exercise is to open the question for wider consideration, but not without prejudice. In the discussion, the western Canadian setting in which this essay is written serves well to highlight several important aspects.

As the reader will readily discover, undergirding the latter part of this essay is a small but very useful and insightful English publication, issued in 1977 by Grove Publications. Entitled *Lay Presidency at the Eucharist?*, it is edited by Trevor Lloyd and includes articles by the editor, Colin Buchanan, Douglas Davies and Robin Nixon. ATR readers will recognize some of these writers, particularly Professor Buchanan, as representatives of the evangelical strand of English Anglicanism.[1]

Circumstances Giving Rise to the Question

The first context to name is the theological-liturgical setting in which the church finds itself at present. In every part of the Anglican Communion, and indeed in the church even more broadly defined, the liturgical assembly is increasingly becoming a eucharistic assembly. This means that the church is moving more and more toward actually practicing what it has for many years claimed as its liturgical norm, that is, weekly eucharist. (In fact, it is sometimes said that we are approaching the point where only the eucharist is to be viewed as authentic Christian worship, surely an inappropriate conclusion.)

Given this broad general trend and the increased need for someone to preside as the church gathers in this setting, it is not difficult to enumerate circumstances in which the matter of the presider could arise.[2]

The most obvious case is that in which the priest is ill or absent and no other ordained person is available as a substitute. This is a common enough occurrence that it requires no further comment. Secondly, there is the situation in which the ordained person is charged with the care of a multi-point parish of such size that regular, every Sunday visits are not possible. An extreme yet not uncommon example of this situation occurs in the Diocese of Cariboo in central British Columbia. The priest in Lytton, B.C., at the confluence of the Thompson and Fraser Rivers, is responsible for 16 points, three white congregations and 13 composed of Native People. No attempt is made by the priest to visit each point each Sunday. Such is also frequently the case in farther northern British Columbia and the Yukon. There priests serve sections of the Alaska

Highway to the extent of as much as 250 miles each. Clearly, if weekly eucharistic celebrations became the norm, the question of eucharistic presidency would be a central issue. Even the matter of weekly visitation by an ordained person is currently unmanageable!

The particular parochial setting used in the preceding illustration points us to another circumstance in which our question might arise. For those who minister in an ethnic community, the matter of the appropriateness of a white "European" priest, for example, presiding at the celebration of a community composed entirely of the Inuits comes into question. If the white European is the only ordained person for vast distances, then one can easily see the flowering of interest in the broader question of eucharistic presidency as related to the need for ethnic solidarity.

As a fourth setting, one thinks of the increasingly frequent occurrences of small group communion. This might be a group on retreat, a small house church or some special-occasion group gathered for a conference or other meeting. Although one will rightly ask whether any of these groups properly constitutes a eucharistic community, or whether the eucharist is the necessary or only suitable liturgy for the gathering, nonetheless, these settings, with one ironic exception, do serve as additional contexts in which to ask our over-arching question.[3] The "one ironic exception" to the preceding observation is this: when a group of clergy gathers, in whatever number and for whatever business, it is possible (and common) for the eucharist to be celebrated at the beginning or end of the meeting. Hence, the dilemma of presidency, as we are presenting it, really need not arise. There are more than enough presiders from which to choose! However, given the particular constitution of the Anglican Church (and others as well), if an even larger number of lay folk were to gather, to work even harder at business even more obviously related to the proclamation of the Gospel, they would *not* be free to begin or conclude their deliberations with the eucharist.

To the general trend toward more frequent eucharistic celebrations and the circumstantial contexts already cited, one can add an important current in the church's life that bears on the matter at hand. This current, very much alive in the liturgical life of the Anglican Church, is the enhancement of the role of laity in the liturgy. To put it differently, we are witnessing a laicization (or re-laicization?) of the church's liturgy. As more and more people are licensed to assist in the preparation and distribution of communion, there is a kind of logic that pushes toward asking about the possibility of a lay person presiding. The implications of this possibility will be the focus of more detailed consideration below. For the moment, simply posing the question will suffice.

These contexts, then, give rise to the question, "who presides?," viz., the increasingly eucharistic liturgical life of the church, the absence of a priest due to illness or absence, the difficulty of frequent communion in a multi-point parish, the maintenance of ethnic solidarity, small group communion away from the whole congregation, and the extension of the logic that currently supports the enhancement of lay liturgical ministry. To this point, all the settings noted, which might give rise to our question, have some logical or natural grounding in Anglicanism. At the same time, the church's ecumenical future gives us yet another place to encounter the same issue.

In a way, the question as to who should preside at the eucharistic assembly arises anytime ecumenical conversations take place, since the matter of the recognition of orders inevitably attracts considerable attention. For our purposes, it is sufficient simply to name this fact without having to engage the nettlesome issue of such recognition itself.

In western Canada, the matter of eucharistic presidency arises as the Anglican Church carries on shared ministries with the United Church of Canada, in recent years a not uncommon reality. The United Church is the product of a 1925 merger of the Methodist, Congregationalist and part of the Presbyterian churches of Canada. It should thus be distinguished from the United Church of Christ in the U.S. The United Church of Canada is the second largest Christian church in Canada, following the Roman Catholics. There are roughly twice as many members of the United Church as there are Anglicans. The United and Anglican churches were previously engaged in union talks which ended in 1975 when the Anglicans withdrew from the conversations at the point when the United Church had approved the proposed Plan of Union. Even though union talks have failed, conversations continue between the two denominations on the mutual recognition of ordained ministries.

In polity, the United Church is presbyterial. As a part of the ordering of the church, it is possible for a conference of the United Church to license and thus authorize a person to the work of lay supply. This, in turn, allows this person to undertake the full (though temporary) expression of congregational ministry, including the exercise of sacramental ministry. This fact, then, bears on the Anglican Church in those places where a shared ministry is undertaken between Anglican and United congregations. These shared ministries, of which there have been many over the last decade in British Columbia, take many and varied form, with buildings, congregations and/or clergy being the "shared" aspect.

Oftentimes, the ordained leadership of these shared ministries alternates between the two denominations. This means that both denominations authorize, by license or otherwise, the duly appointed minister of whichever denomination to function on behalf of both churches. By so doing, when an Anglican bishop licenses a United Church minister, the question of recognition of ordination is set aside.

The situation can arise, however, in which the United Church, in its turn, might appoint a lay supply to serve a joint congregation as an interim appointment. In quite a direct way, then, the eucharistic presidency question is put in a central place, it "insinuates itself into Anglican consciousness," as we put it earlier.

Having completed our exploration of contexts, it should be clear by this point that the posing of the question "who presides?" is not an artificial exercise. On the contrary, the question, given the chance to present itself, is readily available for serious consideration.

One "Answer" to the Question: Sacramental Priests

For many Anglicans, as we said at the outset, the answer to the question "who presides?" will be constant and invariable. Whatever be the context or extraordinary circumstance, it is the priest who presides. In saying this, it is clearly understood that the priest is a theologically trained graduate of a theological school, duly ordained by rightful episcopal authority to exercise "the ministry of a priest in the Church of God" for life (with proper episcopal authorization or licensing). In addition, although priests are to be attached to some identifiable ecclesial unit, e.g., parish, diocese, school, hospital, etc., there is, nonetheless, a geographically universal character to this ordination. That is, this priestly ordering is recognized as valid elsewhere and can be exercised, with episcopal permission, elsewhere.[4]

Important variations in the details of this "standard" answer come to our attention in a significant and precedent-setting instance. In this case, the presider, though a priest, is not the priest of the "standard" answer. The sacramental priests or "sacramentalists," as they are called, are an innovation brought into existence out of what is probably best viewed as a kind of missionary strategy, forged in the face of economic and social need.

In the early 1970s, following the passage in 1969 of Title III, Canon 8 of the national canons of the Episcopal Church, the Diocese of Alaska began to consider and then implement a plan to ordain persons to function as sacramental priests.[5] As reported by William Gordon, the then Bishop of Alaska, Canon 8 has enabled a number of Alaskan communities to select persons from their own midst to be ordained, following minimal training, to the sacramental ministry of the church. This ministry is strictly limited to the sacraments and includes no preaching or teaching beyond that associated with the ministry of any other Christian. It is implicit in these ordinations that the sacramentalists are essentially place-bound, meaning that should a sacramental priest relocate, leaving the originating and ordaining community, the sacramental ministry of that person is discontinued or set aside, to be taken up again only by episcopal invitation and the appropriate episcopal authorization. (In some ways, this latter is not unlike the circumstances of persons ordered priests in the more traditional sense.) Other U.S. dioceses have followed Alaska's lead and benefited from Alaska's experience, e.g., Nevada, Utah, and Eastern Oregon.

The Eucharistic Assembly

The Canadian Church, lacking the enabling canon, has not undertaken anything resembling the Alaska action. Both the dioceses of Keewatin, overlapping Western Ontario and eastern Manitoba, and Caledonia, in northern British Columbia, have ordained as priests candidates chosen largely by tribal councils of elders or villages, but these persons have been more fully trained and then ordained to full priestly ministry without the restrictions of the Alaska plan.

The strengths of the sacramental priests as one answer to our primary question, "who presides?," are several. Firstly, and most obviously, the sacramental life of the church is continued under circumstances in which it might have stopped. Secondly, the ordaining of sacramentalists keeps together and intact the traditional association of priest and presider. Insofar as this is so, there is no alteration in the ordering of the church. Thirdly, the Alaska plan obviously honors the initiative of the local (often ethnic) community. Fourthly, it can be argued that, to the extent that the authority of the priesthood is obviously derived from episcopal ministry, priesthood is an effective sign of that prior episcopal ministry. In this derivative sense, then, the sacramentalist manifests episcopal ministry as priest-in-community.

In addition to all these, the most commonly cited virtue of this "answer" is that it intends to facilitate the assorted ministries of other members of the Christian community, rather than to appear to concentrate them all in one person. Thus, while the liturgical ministry would be done by the sacramentalist, the teaching, administrative, evangelistic, pastoral, and other ministries would be distributed amongst others with gifts to undertake them. (This view is useful in distinguishing the sacramentalists from the mass priests of a previous and, thank God, by-gone era.[6])

A Second "Answer": Lay Presidency

Whereas the ordaining of sacramental priests is a part of the Anglican experience, the suggestion that, in any of the circumstances described earlier, a lay person might preside at the eucharistic assembly comes as a rather more innovative proposal. So far as this writer knows, there is no publication in North American Anglican circles comparable in intent to the near-pamphlet *Lay Presidency at the Eucharist?*, generated from English evangelical sources nearly five years ago. Given the general parochialism of Anglicans, the fact that lay presidency is practiced by other bodies of Christians (read: some Protestants) counts for little as an influence upon us.

It is also important to note that the sacramentalists are ordained as a permanent response to at least some of the problematic circumstances which give rise to the question, "who presides?" This is particularly true in those cases where distance and ethnicity have combined to make the ordaining of indigenous leaders the most responsible solution. To look at lay presidency is to consider a rather different solution in circumstances which arise in a different setting. (At the same time, if lay presidency were to be counted a valid expression of Anglican liturgical order, it might be a useful alternative to sacramentalists in some situations.)

By definition, lay presidency of the eucharistic assembly is to be understood as an occasional, possibly even emergency occurrence, done only after authorization by the bishop and with the support and concurrence of the specific congregation involved. In this regard, the lay presider would be distinguished from the sacramental priests. It would also be characteristic of lay presidency that the authorization could be time and place bound.

We turn now to some of the broader questions implied by the proposal of lay presidency. Because its integrity may be less clear on the surface, some deliberate exposition in support of the suggestion seems appropriate. There can be no argument about the tradition supporting the presidency of the ordained person. It is certainly the norm for the assorted traditions which contain the vast number of Christians both now and in the past. Whatever be one's theology of ordination, be it ontological, functional, or representational, the ordering of the church's liturgical life has traditionally been around the ministry of the ordained.

But the reiteration of this tradition needs to be done with care and without prejudice. Clarity on the matter of eucharistic presidency does not emerge in our history for a rather long time. As A. E. Harvey asserts and Bernard Cooke makes clear, the evidence in the New Testament would *not* support exclusive claims for the eucharistic presidency of the ordained. As Cooke puts it, one of the things that can be said "with fair certitude" is "that there is no clear New Testament indication about the ministry of liturgical leadership."[7] One searches Acts or Paul's writings in vain for substantiation of the tradition of ordained presidency, and that in the face of the indisputable fact that with frequency our forebears did, indeed, share "the breaking of the bread."

Beyond the New Testament, whereas *I Clement* and the Ignatian correspondence might be usable to support exclusive ordained presidency, the *Didache* and Justin's *First Apology* would not.[8] When the Didachist allows the prophets (as distinct from presbyters or bishops) to preside and pray spontaneously at the eucharist, the Didachist is using what for later generations would count as a non-traditional, "non-ordained" category.[9] And certainly Justin's phrase "the president of the brethren" abets almost any arguing point on the question.[10] With Hippolytus in the early third century one finally encounters the recognizable tradition. Here episcopal, or in a derivative sense presbyterial, presidency is the clear norm. For those of catholic heritage, this norm remains in place.

Thus, at the historically descriptive level, it is true to say, *at least,* that we cannot be certain that ordained presidency has always been thought necessary to the definition of the church as a liturgical or eucharistic community. That being so at the descriptive level, should it be argued that ordained presidency *ought to be* necessary or essential to the definition? To put the matter differently, in the absence of a priest is it not possible for the church to celebrate the eucharist? Response to this question sets in motion a mixture of important theological and sociological (or practical) issues.

The most important theological clue to the answer to the question as posed is the recognition, now common to the church, that the action of the eucharistic assembly is the action of *the community as a whole* rather than the action of any given individual. The presider facilitates, enables, animates, focuses the eucharistic action of the whole community. This view sets the reality of the church as a prior condition for the reality of liturgical presidency, rather than the other way round. It also sets Christian initiation as the constituent element for the eucharistic community rather than ordination.[11] The liturgy is by definition the common and participatory activity of the gathered community and no one's private or exclusive domain.

At the same time, and necessarily so, both symbolic needs and the need for order must be satisfied if the eucharistic assembly is to be who it claims to be, i.e., the Body of Christ. The priest stands in the midst of the community as both sign and agent of the community's gathering and actions. "The ordained ministry is a sign of the Church's unity and continuity with the whole Catholic Church and the apostolic tradition. The presidency of the ordained person at the eucharist, therefore, signifies not only the unity of the local community in its gathering for the central acts of its life, but also its unity and continuity with the whole church in its proclamation and celebration of the Word in both its historical and world-wide sense."[12]

Thus, when Trevor Lloyd puts the question as if unanswerable, "If it is the whole community gathered around the Lord's Table which celebrates the eucharist, what is the function of the president?,"[13] the answer comes back, if the presider is an ordained person, a very basic and necessary sign function is accomplished for and with the community. And, we might add, being realistic, if one imagines the eucharistic presider as a non-ordained person, this sign function is not so fully accomplished, given our continual association of apostolicity and catholicity with ordination rather than with baptism. In addition to the priest's sign function, it is also this person who attests to and, indeed, effects for a specific congregation, the ordering of the church's life. (It is this fact which makes less helpful the ordaining of persons as sacramentalists, accomplishing as this does the dislocation of liturgical ordering from the total ordering of the church.)

The ordering question, however, needs to be pursued. Is any body properly ordered if the absence of one member disables the basic functioning of the whole assembly? A. E. Harvey, to whom we have already referred, offers the analogy of a chairperson presiding at the board meeting of a complex institution, a person who by experience and insight is best able to oversee the actions and decision-making of the board. Yet, that board will also recognize the necessity of doing its business even should its chairperson be absent. In that case, some appropriate deputy will be asked to take the chair. Harvey writes, "the order and efficiency of the institution is safeguarded so long as the officers are normally present to fulfil their tasks . . . Order is threatened only if the absences become habitual or are complacently accepted." [14]

The analogy suggests that it is the group's actions that are essential rather than the persistent presence of any given actor. The validity of this point is intensified in the liturgical situation, in which we are increasingly aware that the celebrant is the community, not the presider.

Since it is most unlikely in most congregations that there will be an ordained person available to serve as the priest's "deputy" in the liturgy in the priest's absence, does this necessarily mean that the assembly cannot be about its proper business? It seems more reasonable and responsible to suggest that an episcopally authorized lay "deputy" might stand in the normal presider's place on those (presumably rare) occasions when the need arises. With such authorization and the controls that such authorization suggests, the church would surely experience no loss of order.

On this premise, then, occasional episcopally authorized lay presidency would be an appropriate answer to the question which initiated this essay, viz., "who presides?"

A Final Comment

This essay has attempted to demonstrate that the question "who presides?" arises in its own circumstances with integrity and not artificially. The two answers discussed are probably only two of some several others that escape notice at the moment. The attempt has been made to present these two answers in such a way as to make them credible responses to the question on a theological basis, responses that one might choose or accept for theological reasons. It has been indirectly suggested that these two answers, in their respective ways, might be "right" answers to the question, given the proper circumstances and cautions. The shortcomings of even these "right" answers will be variously identified by assorted readers and critics.

At the same time, it is appropriate and necessary to admit that what most often moves the church to explore and then (sometimes) to do what is "right" theologically is not the persuasive power of theological argumentation but rather the necessities imposed by the economic realities of our time. This is not to speak from a cynical point of view so much as to speak realistically about the experience of the church in the present age. Some have the habit, in the face of such evidence, of wishing that the church had had the vision to act for theological reasons *before* economic pressure brought action, action which many might describe as the good thing that could have been done earlier, for "better" reasons. Yet, it seems incontestably true, for example, that congregations have merged for their good and the good of the Gospel *because of economic pressure,* that diocesan structures have changed (improved) *because of economic pressure,* that theological curricula have been strengthened and made more useful *because of economic pressure,* that church buildings have been made more human, social places rather than museums *because of economic pressure,* that ministry has been made more directly relevant to the lives of people *because of economic pressure,* and so it goes.

Consequently, one may have reason to think that any impetus that might mount behind the "answers" noted in this essay will likely come because of economic pressure. This seems the case in the Alaska situation, begun over ten years ago and duplicated and strengthened elsewhere in the meantime. It is economics that moves us (at least sometimes) toward goals that are most appropriate for us, and for the proclamation of the Gospel. And, being moved, even slightly, in the direction of the poor seems to help re-acquaint us with the Good News that the poor expect to hear from the church.

In this light, it may well be that in the near future some economic pressure will move the church to a more serious consideration of the enormous substance of lay ministry, even the lay ministry of liturgical presidency. It may well be that this successful economic pressure, discernable in so many instances, will finally be recognizable to us as the more devious side of God's graciousness to the church.

---

1. This essay was originally published in the *Anglican Theological Review.*

2. I have chosen to use the term "presider" rather than "president" even though I find it in some ways a less felicitous term. "Presider" seems to avoid the political implications (and confusion) of "president." At the same time, "presidency" is inescapable. "Presider" also leaves more open the relative permanence of the appointment, a question related to the matter at hand. I am influenced in this regard by Robert Hovda in *Strong, Loving and Wise* (Washington, D.C.: The Liturgical Conference, 1976), although Hovda contrasts "presider" with "celebrant" rather than with "president."

3. Lloyd, *Lay Presidency . . . ?*, p. 4, proposes yet another setting, viz., the eucharistic ministry to the sick or housebound. This would be a suitable addition to the list only if it were argued that the entirety of the eucharistic liturgy were to be celebrated in the sickroom. If the reserved sacrament were used, which one suspects (hopes) is most common, then the delivery of communion would be an obvious extension of the celebration of the whole community and, thus, would *not* necessarily raise questions about who presides in the sickroom.

4. One must be quick to admit that in the various dioceses of the Anglican Church of Canada, not all bishops ordain and/or recognize the ordinations of women to priestly orders. Hence, some dioceses would put in question the geographical portability of a woman's priesthood.

5. Details of this action are sketched briefly by William J. Gordon, Jr., the then Bishop of Alaska, in "The Church in Alaska—its mission and development," in *The Living Church*, 168/10 (March 10, 1974), pp. 9–10. I am indebted to David Cochran, Bishop Gordon's successor and only recently retired from the episcopal office in Fairbanks, for materials and insights so readily shared with me.

6. See, for example, Robert Anderson, "Changing Concepts of Ministry—One Story," *Coalition 14 Papers*, 1979.

7. Cooke, *Ministry to Word and Sacrament* (Philadelphia: Fortress Press, 1976), p. 529; Harvey, *Priest or President?* (London: SCK, 1975), p. 45.

8. On the other hand, Harvey argues that both Clement and Ignatius are not saying that the eucharist "*cannot* be celebrated by anyone else, but rather

that it *ought not* to be if proper order is to be maintained in the Church." *Ibid.,* pp. 45–46.

9. *Didache*, x, 7.

10. Justin's *First Apology*, 65, 67.

11. One wishes that debates about the catholicity or apostolicity of the church had to do more with baptism than with ordination, thus avoiding the persistent and indefensible equation of clergy with church.

12. These are the words of my colleague, W.R.K. Crockett, taken from an unpublished report he presented to the Anglican Church of Canada's Doctrine and Worship Committee summarizing for the Committee's benefit a report called "Project Ministry" prepared by the United Church of Canada. Used with his kind permission.

13. "Introduction," *Lay Presidency* . . . ?, p. 9.

14. Previously cited, p. 47.

Chapter Five

Given and Shed for Whom?
A Study of the Words of Administration

Mine is the experience of other Anglicans, of whatever nationality. Until very recent years, each time I received the eucharistic elements I heard these words:

The Body of our Lord Jesus Christ, which was given for thee, preserve thy body and soul unto everlasting life:

Take and eat this in remembrance that Christ died for thee, and feed on him in thy heart by faith with thanksgiving.

The Blood of our Lord Jesus Christ, which was shed for thee, preserve thy body and soul unto everlasting life:

Drink this in remembrance that Christ's blood was shed for thee and be thankful.[1]

If I listened carefully, I learned that the Body and Blood of Jesus were given and shed "for thee," i.e., for me. This same statement was made to others who knelt or stood beside me. Each of us was told that the sacrifice of Christ was offered by him for each of us.

Somewhere, in the midst of the liturgical revising that now characterizes the life of the churches, I began to have second thoughts about this durable and oft-repeated eucharistic assertion. I have now come to the conclusion that this assertion is at least misleading and may be altogether false. This essay is partially a consequence of my "second thoughts." The other motivation is an increased concern to urge upon the church more inclusive language, a concern typically raised by opponents of sexist liturgical language (among which I count myself), but suitably raised in other contexts as well.

In undertaking to examine these words of administration, two purposes are being served—one, survey, and the other, discussion. The structure of the essay is as follows: firstly, a brief historical section will survey the language of eucharistic distribution to the time of the Reformation and only slightly beyond. In such a survey, particular attention will be paid to the emergence of the words of administration used in the early editions of the Book of Common Prayer. The second part of the essay will attempt to argue *against* the language used in this formula to declare the atonement "fact" to each communicant. This argument is the center of the essay. In the final section, we will collect and examine the assorted administration forms that characterize a broad range of revisions, offering observations which take their genesis from the second part of the essay. The reader should be clear that the focal concern here is specifically a "two-word problem"—"for thee/you (singular)." Concern for older arguments about presence or aspects of sacrifice are not at issue here. Indeed, one hopes that they have been put to rest for a while.

Lastly, by way of introduction, one other thing should be said. Given the existence of a large number of "permanent revisions," i.e., revisions that committees undoubtedly hope will endure for a time, it may seem unkind to raise the following concerns now, rather than, say, a decade ago. Indeed, I wish they had been raised then, but, so far as I can determine, they were not.

A Brief Historical Review

The history of the words of administration (or distribution) has yet to be written. In this short compass we can do no more than offer a rather bold outline. Such a sampling, however, will help to inform what follows and, indeed, makes its own point well enough.

The earliest example of words of administration comes to us in the *Apostolic Tradition* of Hippolytus. Of the two eucharistic rites recounted in this text, only the baptismal eucharist contains an account of the actual distribution. (The eucharist following the ordination of the bishop contains no instruction.) At the reception of the bread, the following is to be said, "The Bread of Heaven in Christ Jesus." Then follows the reception of the three cups, the first of water, the second of milk and honey, the third of wine. Each cup is tasted three times, during which a trinitarian formula is recited, "In God the Father Almighty . . . And in the Lord Jesus Christ . . . And in the Holy Spirit and in the Holy Church." The communicant is instructed to say "Amen" following each phrase.[2] (This participation and affirmation by the recipient was an important aspect in the communion and, as many will recognize, has returned in many contemporary revisions.) Since this formula is used in the *Apostolic Tradition* on the occasion of a baptism, when the newly baptized are receiving the eucharist for the first time—a circumstance conceivably requiring special language—we can only speculate as to what might have been used at another eucharist.[3]

Other early sources provide other examples, suggesting as they do a certain diversity across the church. In the *Apostolic Constitutions*, Book VIII, the formula is very simple. With the bread the priest says, "The Body of Christ," and with the cup, "The Blood of Christ, the cup of Life." Again, following each reception, the communicant says, "Amen."[4] Later, the Mozarabic Rite provides these words, "The body of our Lord Jesus Christ be your salvation" and "The blood of Christ remain with you as true redemption."[5] The early Roman Rite contains these words, "The body of our Lord Jesus Christ keep your soul in eternal life," and "The blood of our Lord Jesus Christ keep your soul in eternal life."[6]

Even so scant a sampling suggests the range of language which would typify (at least in the West) the distribution of the eucharistic elements prior to the sixteenth century. No set form was universal. Indeed, as Joseph Jungmann suggested, "Every member of the traditional schema has its variants."[7] More often than not, however, the emphasis was that of the Pauline and Synoptic sources (the body and blood of Christ) rather than the Johannine references to the bread of heaven (John 6:31.). Also, it seems clear that the delivery of the elements, however infrequently as time passed, was to persons who came forward to the altar to receive. Only to the sick and infirm would any other pattern of delivery be used.

Looking now at the sixteenth century Reformation, it is demonstrably clear that assorted eucharistic issues gave great impetus to the reformers' zeal. Among the many places in which these issues manifest themselves we could count the words used at the distribution of the bread and wine. In fact, it is as a consequence of the concerns of the reformers that the words of administration took on new theological importance. The reformers' concerns about presence and sacrifice could not help finding expression at the time of distribution. In addition, the reformers' preoccupation with Scripture was to have clear impact on the issue under consideration here.

Luther's revisions of the Mass were the *Formula Missae* (1523) and the *Deutsche Messe* (1526). Although there is no stipulation of words of administration in the German mass, the *Formula Missae* contains the words of the Roman Rite, "The body (blood) of our Lord Jesus Christ preserve your soul unto everlasting life." Luther's conservative nature, liturgically speaking, was not shared by his successors. Before turning our attention to those later Lutheran sources, however, a look at Zwingli's rite is necessary.

Zwingli's "revision" of 1925, *Action or Use of the Lord's Supper,* indicates significant changes from the medieval pattern. Firstly, the bread and wine are to be carried to the recipients, who are sitting "about the choir."[8] Secondly, there are no words of distribution. Rather, the narrative of the institution is to be read just prior to the distribution.[9]

The German developments following Luther and the later work done by Calvin (based largely on the work of Martin Bucer in Strasbourg) evidence an increased interest in the words of institution as derived primarily from Paul's narration in I Corinthians 11. This interest is incorporated into the inherited (medieval) pattern for distribution and finds its way into the English revisions of 1548 and 1549. For the purposes of the present essay, this incorporation is of particular importance.

Beginning as early as 1525 and certainly by the early 1530's, a particular tendency toward individualization in the words of administration is in evidence.[10] It is important to note, at the same time, that some forms of individualization had already been manifest, as we have seen before. Jungmann presents yet another formula, this one reaching back to the eighth century, which reads, "May the Body and Blood of our Lord Jesus Christ preserve thee unto life everlasting."[11] This kind of individualization is a blessing form, aimed at the application of a blessing upon a given person. The individualization attendant upon the sixteenth century change is of a different sort.

In the Brandenburg-Nurnberg Church Order (1533), the distribution is accomplished with these words, "Take and eat, this is the body of Christ which is given for thee," and "Take and drink, this is the blood of the new Testament, which is shed for thy sins."[12] In Martin Bucer's Strasbourg rite dating from the end of the next decade, 1539, the words are "Remember, believe and proclaim that Christ the Lord has died for you." The distribution was made to communicants who knelt at the step in front of the Table (unlike Zwingli).[13] In the same Bucerian lineage is the Church Order of Cologne, written at the invitation of the Archbishop, Hermann von Wied, in 1543. In *A Simple and Religious Consultation* (English translation 1547) are found the following, "Take and eat to thy health the body of the Lord, which was delivered for thee (*für dich*)," and "Take and drink to thy health the blood of the Lord, which was shed for thy sins."[14] This is the form that most immediately influenced the English forms.

Calvin's revision of 1542, *The Form of Church Prayers and Hymns*, contains no words of administration, only the rubrical instruction that "Scripture be read during the distribution" (The distribution was accomplished by having people come forward to receive). The second edition, however, dated 1545, contained the following formula for distribution, "Take, eat, the body of Jesus which was delivered unto death for thee (*vous*)" and "This is the cup of the new testament in the blood of Jesus which has been shed for you (*vous*)."[15] Although apparently ambiguous, the "vous" is rightly understood as the plural rather than formal singular. When John Knox used this same language it was clearly intended as a plural.[16]

As is now becoming clear, as the words of institution adapted from I Corinthians found their way into the formula of distribution, particularly the German revisions, an interesting change occurred. The collective and plural "you" of Paul's narrative often became a singular "you."[17] A subtle and most significant shift! In the past, the giving of the elements might have been accomplished by an assertion of the individual *appropriation* of the divine action, e.g., Jungmann's example, " . . . preserve thee unto life everlasting." With the introduction of the narrative of institution into the occasion of distribution, the wording suggested that the divine action had been aimed at or undertaken on behalf of particular individuals. It is to this very concern that we will return later.

At this point the English revisions must engage our attention.[18] The Order of Communion (1548) was the first revision offered by Thomas Cranmer. Issued just prior to the production of the first Book of Common Prayer (1549), the Order was in English and was inserted in the Latin Mass. This Order contained the following words of administration, "The Body of our Lord Jesus Christ, which was given for thee, preserve thy body unto eternal life," and "The blood of our Lord Jesus Christ, which was shed for thee, preserve thy soul to eternal life."[19] Clearly, the Continental Lutheran influence is demonstrated in the phrases "given for thee" and "shed for thee." In addition, Cranmer's formula demonstrates the then current assumption which related the efficacy of the bread to the life of the body and that of the wine to the life of the soul. This view is a duplicate of the language of the Prayer of Humble Access which preceded the distribution, "That our sinful bodies may be made clean by his body, and our souls washed through his most precious blood."[20]

Following the 1548 Order, the first Book of Common Prayer abandoned the dualistic assumption in the words of administration, adding to each statement the words necessary to achieve balance, "preserve thy body and soul unto everlasting life." With this change, the eventual forms of the English words of administration are almost reached.

To the revisers of the 1549 book, the original words of administration seemed to associate the presence of Christ rather too closely with the elements themselves. In place of these earlier words, a memorialist alternative was proposed, "Take and eat this, in remembrance that Christ died for thee, and feed on him in thy heart by faith, with thanksgiving," and "Drink this in remembrance that Christ's blood was shed for thee, and be thankful."

From the point of view of the present study, one needs to note with particular care not only the change of language but also the intensification of the individualization in the language. This intensification was augmented all the more with the decision made in the 1559 BCP issued after the accession of Elizabeth. In a typically Anglican maneuver, the words of the 1549 book were combined with those of 1552. Thus, at the time of receiving the bread and wine (and certainly depending on the pace at which the words were spoken), the communicant might very well hear four times (twice each for the bread and wine) that the actions of Christ in giving his body and shedding his blood were "for thee."

The language of the Elizabethan Prayer Book has characterized the assorted Anglican revisions ever since, until very recently. Beyond the Anglican usage, the 1559 formula has influenced other English language rites, most notably John Wesley's Sunday Morning Service (1784), in which the words of administration of the Book of Common Prayer are (not surprisingly) reproduced without modification.[21]

The consequence of this history, even so sketchily drawn, is that the received tradition for many English speaking Christians—Anglicans, Methodists, and Lutherans in particular—contains the assertion that the sacrifice of Christ was offered "for thee/you (singular)." This assertion has been repeated at eucharists for centuries to millions of faithful people.

The Heart of the Matter

The tracing of the broader dimensions of the history of these words of administration only provides a context for examining the theological claims and interpretations affirmed and set in motion by them. My intention, as admitted at the outset, is to argue *against* the use of the words "for thee/you (singular)" at the moment of receiving the elements and, having argued thus, to look at the language of some of the current revisions. Before doing so, however, it seems appropriate to present as clearly as possible the views of those who have spoken pointedly in favor of the words "for thee/you (singular)," words which derive from the sixteenth century Anglican and Lutheran revisions.

In the earliest phases of the current revision process in the Episcopal Church, the Standing Liturgical Commission began issuing a series of *Prayer Book Studies,* number four of which was called "The Eucharistic Liturgy." In making recommendations about the words of administration to be used in any forthcoming revision, the authors wrote:

> We propose as Sentences of Administration the first twelve words of Cranmer's formula of 1549: "The Body of our Lord Jesus Christ, which was given for thee," and "The Blood of our Lord Jesus Christ, which was shed for thee." This is short enough for individual use. It is a statement of the basic reality, without homiletical additions of any sort. Moreover, it is a perfectly balanced form: it combines the Catholic "Corpus Domini nostri Jesu Christi" of the Latin Mass, with the Protestant "der für dich gegeben ist" and "das für deine Sunde vergossen ist" of Hermann of Cologne. This *individual* [emphasis theirs] emphasis is of great importance in Anglican thought, and the most "Catholic minded" member of the Church would feel his devotion impoverished if he were deprived of it. If each of us can realize the fact that the Body and Blood of Christ have been given for *me* [emphasis theirs], then any added phrases become superfluous—at least at this vital instant.[22]

Though taking a somewhat more moderate position on the matter of individualization, other writers have tended to make the same point.[23]

The issue at hand is not whether the sacrament is a means of grace for individual communicants. The appropriation of the divine action through sacramental power is always specific. Rather, the question relates to the aim, intention and direction of the divine action. Without wanting to engage a full debate as to whether Christ's atoning death should be spoken of as having occurred "on behalf of," or "instead of," or "for" X, I want to suggest that Christ's atoning death did *not* occur on behalf of, or instead of, or for *individuals* but rather for *a collection of persons whose primary identity is that collection rather than their own individuality.* This being the case, to say at the communion, e.g., that Christ's blood was shed for me, would be to misrepresent to me at a very "vital instant" what God has in fact done.

Instead, what I need to know without qualification is this: that the action of God in Christ for the many is efficacious for me.

As the best and only necessary premise for this view, consider the language of the New Testament:

> Just as the Son of Man came not to be served but to serve and to give his life as a ransom *for many.* (Mt 20.28: cf. Mk 10.45)
> . . . so Christ, having been offered once to bear the sins of *many* . . . (Heb 9.28)
> . . . for this is my blood of the covenant, which is poured out *for many* for the forgiveness of sins. (Mt 26.28; cf. Mk 14.24)

> For there is one God, and there is also one mediator between God and humankind, Jesus Christ, himself human, who gave himself a ransom *for all* . . . (I Tim 2.5f.)
> He who did not withhold his own Son, but gave him up *for all of us,* will he not with him also give us everything else? (Rom 8.32) [24]

The impact and aim of this language is clear. Without needing to settle the question of the limits of the corporate image, we ought certainly to affirm the corporate nature of the atoning act of God in Christ.

When, however, someone presses the question as to the "collective" for whom Christ died (if taken to be less than "all"), the issues become more complicated. Is the community of the atonement the community of the church? Is the *koinonia* that is created by partaking of the Body and Blood of Christ also the *koinonia* of the atonement? [25] As tantalizing as these speculations are, for the purposes of the present essay no answer is required. Our concern is finally not with the question "which collective?" but rather with the affirmation that the atonement is more properly understood as a collective and corporate doctrine than an individual one.

One of the most interesting facets of biblical anthropology is that suggested by the notion of corporate personality. In an insightful article, Philip Kaufman calls to mind some valuable and important observations.[26] Particularly, as regards Paul's writing in Romans 5, Kaufman holds up for us the fact that in Christ we are all contained. We are all represented/personified/contained within him in his death and rising. This means that *prior to* our individual point of reference we have the corporate point of reference in Christ.

Some will conclude that to argue thus is to argue in favor of the depersonalization of the faith/church/liturgy. This is not the case. Instead, and on the contrary, my plea would be that we re-envision ourselves in corporate terms. To share in the *corpus* for which Christ died, to be in the *corpus* which is contained in Christ's corporate personality, ought to be and ought to be understood to be a very personal (though not individual) status—corporate and personal but not individual and private.

An interesting and appropriate amplification of this line of argument is provided by Herman Schmidt. Writing in *Studia Liturgica,* on the subject "Language and its Function in Christian Worship," Schmidt observed that since "the liturgy is an activity of a community, its language must be a community-language."[27] He went on to suggest that because the language of worship is the language of the "engagement" of the community with God and the world, it is personal language *by not being individual;* that is, "personal" is to be understood as a corporate rather than individual quality. Once made individual, the language becomes the language of *dis*engagement with the language-community in which one is a *person.*[28]

From this premise, we can return to the two words that precipitated this discussion, "for thee/you (singular)." Given the line of thinking just concluded, it is clear that a liturgical statement which suggests that the atonement occurred for me is at best misleading. This is particularly so when, as is the case in some informal eucharists I have attended in recent years, the words of administration contain not only the statement that I am receiving the body and blood which were given and shed for me, but also contained my own given name, e.g., "The Body of Christ, given for you, Bill." This particularity is unacceptable.[29]

The Standing Liturgical Commission of the Episcopal Church has called the moment of reception "a vital instant." That is most appropriate language; it is a moment at which life is indeed present and available. It is a "personal" instant. Consequently, it is precisely the instant for each of us to be told about our relatedness and corporateness in Christ and not about our individuality. My appropriation of what Christ effected is a function of my relatedness—not the other way around. Thus, it would be most appropriate for me to hear the minister of communion say, "This is the Body of Christ which was given for many/all, take this and eat it." Honesty and faithfulness require the rehearsal of a corporate fact in a most personal way.[30]

Surely this is ample evidence to affirm the corporate nature of what our Lord gave and did for humankind. And, by the grace of God, we receive it, each and all, as a gift in the eucharist. Consequently, my conviction is that this corporate fact ought to be represented in our words of administration, or at the very least the opposite claim should not be made.

Perhaps an analogy will serve to conclude this argument. If a family were to receive a gift, it would be inappropriate (and perhaps inaccurate) for any member of the family to say, "The gift was given to me." What makes the family member a recipient of the gift is that person's membership in or relatedness to the group (family). This relatedness is a prior condition to the appropriation of the benefits of the gift by any particular family member. This is to say, "The gift was given to the family of which I am a part and I myself may use it or benefit from it." So it is, also, I have argued, with the sacrifice of Christ.

The words of F. J. Leenhardt will serve to conclude this section. "The merciful purpose of Christ embraces the many, and no one can believe, without violating the love thus manifested, that he alone is accepted by Christ by virtue of privilege. When Christ offers me the bread, I participate in an action which is provided for all. And not only am I associated with those by my side, but I am also united to all those who, with me, are the object of the life-giving sacrifice of the cross." [31]

Contemporary Examples

From the foregoing, it might appear that I mean to prescribe this set of words as the only ones for use at the eucharist. This is certainly not the case. Rather, I mean only to suggest that if this formula is to be used—as it frequently is—it needs to be re-thought and re-stated. Instead of arguing for one formula (which would surely be an ineffectual argument) we are wiser to look at the variety of administrative practices currently available among the revisions of the several churches. Much of the accumulated eucharistic heritage of the church is evidenced in such a survey.

The simplest and most straightforward formula is that of the Roman Mass. The words are these, "The Body (Blood) of Christ." [32]

The form from the Presbyterian *Worshipbook,* 1970, following a permissive rubric ("may be said"), is composed of two scriptural statements which will function as both invitation and words of distribution.

> Jesus said: "I am the Bread of Life. He who comes to me will never be hungry; he who believes in me will never thirst."
>
> Jesus said: "I am the vine, you are the branches. Cut off from me you can do nothing."

We should recall that the reading of Scripture during the distribution of communion was Calvin's first preference (1542), rather than words of administration.

The *Lutheran Book of Worship* contains three rites for the eucharist. In each rite, the following serve as the words of administration: "The Body (Blood) of Christ, given (shed) for you." [33] The Methodist text entitled "The Sacrament of the Lord's Supper, Revised Edition 1981," contains almost exactly the same words, "The Body (Blood) of Christ, given for you."[34] In both these cases, the method of distribution would be that of individual reception by coming forward to the altar/table. Also, in both cases, the statements run afoul of the objections raised in the earlier part of this essay. The sentences would escape criticism only if they were addressed to the whole assembly, the word "you" in each case, thereby, to be understood as a plural (and therefore) collective term.

The *Service Book* of the United Church of Canada (founded in 1925 as a merger of Methodists, Congregationalists and some Presbyterians) contains four orders for the Lord's Supper. In the first, following sentences of invitation said to the assembly ("The body [blood] of Christ broken [shed] for you."), the words of distribution are, "The Body (Blood) of our Lord Jesus Christ keep you unto eternal life." In the second order, following the same invitatory sentences, the bread and cup are given to each with these words, "Jesus Christ, the bread of life," and "Jesus Christ, the true vine." The words which occur in the third order are exactly those which derive from the older BCP formula. The fourth order for the Lord's Supper, designed for informal gatherings, stipulates no particular form of words for administration.[35]

Sentences available for use in Anglican revisions vary widely. Many of the alternatives completely avoid the older Prayer Book form and, consequently, also avoid the problem under consideration. The English, Canadian and American rites, cited here as a sampling, offer alternatives in each of several liturgies.

In the English Holy Communion Rite A, *Alternative Service Book*, the President is directed to say to the assembly:

> Draw near with faith. Receive the body of our Lord Jesus Christ which is given for you, and his blood which he shed for you.
> Eat and drink in remembrance that he died for you, and feed on him in your hearts by faith with thanksgiving.

At the time of reception either of the following (or the 1662 sentences) is to be used:

"The body (blood) of Christ keep you in eternal life" or "The body (blood) of Christ." Communicants are directed to reply, "Amen." [36]

In a variation of Rite A, subtitled "following the pattern of 1662," the words of administration are the traditional ones, although those just above are optional. The optional ones, however, are not printed with this text.

In Holy Communion Rite B, the communion is to be administered in one of two ways. Either the priest uses the traditional formula (to "each communicant," the rubric directs) or the priest says a general declaration to the assembly and a choice of sentences at the actual reception. The general invitation reads as follows:

> Draw near and receive the body of our Lord Jesus Christ which was given for you, and his blood which was shed for you. Take this in remembrance that Christ died for you, and feed on him in your hearts by faith with thanksgiving.

The sentence said at the reception is chosen from these: "The body (blood) of Christ," or "The body (blood) of Christ preserve your body and soul unto everlasting life," or "The body (blood) of our Lord Jesus Christ, which was given (shed) for you, preserve your body and soul unto everlasting life." The communicant is directed to respond "Amen." [37]

Canadian Anglican revisions are contained in the draft *Book of Alternative Services*, formal publication of which will occur in 1985. The *BAS* contains two eucharistic rites. In the first, the presider invites the people by saying, "The gifts of God for the People of God." The people respond, "Thanks be to God." The reception is accompanied by either these formulas: "The body of Christ (given for you)" and "The blood of Christ (shed for you)," or "The body of Christ, the bread of heaven," and "The blood of Christ, the cup of salvation." [38] The parenthesis in the first alternative suggests the optional status of the enclosure and hints, at least, at the compiler's preference for the shorter form. From the point of view of the present essay, the parenthetical option could be dropped.

In the second text, written in the language of the Canadian Book of Common Prayer (1962), the rubrics direct that either the traditional words

Given and Shed for Whom?

be said to each communicant or the following: "The Body of Christ, the bread of heaven" and "The Blood of Christ, the cup of salvation."[39]

Readers of the *ATR* will be familiar with the language of the American BCP.[40] Rite I retains the sentences from 1928 and provides as alternatives the choices available in Rite II, namely,

> The Body (Blood) of our Lord Jesus Christ keep you in everlasting life. [*Amen.*]

> or

> The Body of Christ, the Bread of heaven. [*Amen.*]
> The Blood of Christ, the Cup of salvation. [*Amen.*]

In each case (Rite I or II), the words of administration follow upon a sentence of general invitation, "The Gifts of God for the People of God" to which may be added, "Take them in remembrance that Christ died for you, and feed on him in your heart by faith, with thanksgiving."[41] This addition contains language similar to that of the two general invitations contained in the English *Alternative Service Book* cited earlier. Presumably the "you" in each case is to be understood as a plural form, since the whole assembly is being addressed. At the same time, given the individual interpretation characteristic of the traditional formula of administration, it is conceivable that this same individualistic interpretation is "heard" even when the congregation as a whole is meant to receive the invitation.

Although there are undoubtedly other sources which might be included in our survey, space will not permit. It is also likely that among North American churches most of the alternatives are included in those we have already identified. (The inclusion of the Church of England forms may be justified in that the "problem" addressed in this essay is at least partially of English origin.)

It seems clear from this survey that many formulas for the administration of the eucharistic elements avoid the "two-word" problem that precipitated this essay. They do not continue to assert that Christ died for each individual. At the same time, some continue to make this claim. For Lutherans using the *Lutheran Book of Worship* and Methodists using

"The Sacrament of the Lord's Supper," no alternatives seem available. For others, however, there are formulas which make avoiding the "problem" at least an optional possibility. My earnest hope is that they will take that option, for reasons I hope I have made clear. Certainly Peter Fink is correct in saying, "Whatever creates in the people a sense that they are simply alone before their God speaks a message that is in conflict with the Christian Eucharist." [42]

---

1. The Book of Common Prayer, any edition between the 1559 Elizabethan edition and the current American revision. Although it is the practice of the Anglican churches that sets the context for this article, the evidence suggests that the implications raised are relevant beyond those limits.

2. Geoffrey Cuming (ed.), *Hippolytus: A Text for Students* (Bramcote, Notts, UK: Grove, 1976), chapter 21.

3. Gregory Dix suggests that this threefold formula was used at other occasions for "the partaking of the eucharistic chalice alone." *The Shape of the Liturgy* (London: Adam and Charles Black, 1964), p. 137.

4. R.C.D. Jasper and Geoffrey Cuming, *Prayers of the Eucharist: Early and Reformed* (London: Collins, 1975), pp. 73–74; E.F. Brightman, *Liturgies Eastern and Western* (Oxford: Clarendon Press, 1896), Volume I, p. 25.

5. Jasper and Cuming, previously cited, p. 97.

6. *Ibid.*, p. 110.

7. *Mass of the Roman Rite,* one-volume edition translated by F.A. Brunner, revised by C.K. Riefe (London: Burns and Oates, 1959), p. 514.

8. Yngve Brilioth, *Eucharistic Faith and Practice,* translated by A.G. Hebert (London: SPCK, 1956), p. 161.

9. Jasper and Cuming, previously cited, p. 120; Bard Thompson, *Liturgies of the Western Church* (Cleveland and New York: Meridian Books/World, 1961), p. 154f.

10. E.F. Brightman, *The English Rite* (London: Rivington, 1915), Volume 1, p. lxxv.

11. Previously cited, p. 514.

12. Text appears in Geoffrey Cuming's *A History of Anglican Liturgy* (London and New York: Macmillan and St. Martin's Press, 1969), p. 331.

13. G.J. van de Poll, *Martin Bucer's Liturgical Ideas* (Te Assen: Van Gorcum, 1954), p. 42.

14. Cuming, previously cited, p. 355. Cuming indicates that the phrase "for thee" was changed to "for thy sins" in the 1547 and 1558 English translations. See also Brightman, *The English Rite*, previously cited, Volume 2, p. 700.

15. Brilioth, previously cited, p. 176.

16. W.D. Maxwell, *The Liturgical Portions of the Genevan Service Book* (London: Faith Press, 1965), pp. 137f, 206–209.

17. *Touto mou estin to sōma to hyper hymōn* (I Cor 11:24).

18. Important general sources for the following paragraphs are Brightman, *The English Rite*, previously cited, *passim;* J.H. Srawley, "The Holy Communion Service" in *Liturgy and Worship*, edited by W.K. Lowther Clarke (London: SPCK, 1932), pp. 302–373; and Cuming, previously cited, *passim.*

19. Cuming, previously cited, p. 366.

20. The language of this prayer, if not the underlying assumptions, has persisted in Anglican revisions until the most recent ones, having been a part of the 1928 American and 1962 Canadian books. Is has been removed from the current American revision.

21. Bard Thompson, previously cited, p. 432.

22. The Standing Liturgical Commission [of the Episcopal Church], *Prayer Book Studies IV: The Eucharistic Liturgy* (New York: Church Pension Fund, 1953), p. 285.

23. Luther D. Reed, *The Lutheran Liturgy* (Philadelphia: Muhlenberg, 1947), p. 348; Massey Shepherd, *The Oxford American Prayer Book Commentary* (New York: Oxford University Press, 1950, pp. 82–83; and Charles Smyth, "Communion" in *The Liturgy*, edited by K. MacKenzie (London: SPCK, 1938), pp. 114–127.

24. All citations are from the New Revised Standard Version, emphasis mine. J. Jeremias argues that "while 'many' in Greek (as in English) stands in opposition to 'all,' and therefore has the exclusive sense (*'many, but not all'*), Hebrew *rabbim* can have the inclusive sense (*'the whole, comprising many individuals'*)." *The Eucharistic Words of Jesus*, translated by Norman Perrin (New York: Scribner, 1966), p. 179. He concludes that *pollōn*, "many," is a Semitism and should be read as an inclusive term. *Ibid.*, p. 182.

25. Another complication is introduced into this discussion if one were to suggest that, if the covenant God made with the people of Israel on Sinai has

not been terminated or superseded but continues to this day, then the Christian theological category "atonement" needs to be rethought entirely. (I have obviously bracketed the implications of this suggestion in this essay.)

26. "The One and the Many: Corporate Personality," *Worship* 42:546–548.

27. "Language and Its Function in Christian Worship," *Studia Liturgica* 8:1–25.

28. *Ibid.*, p. 11.

29. Jungmann gives precedent for the practice of naming the recipient but in connection with administrative sentences of a different sort. *The Mass of the Roman Rite*, previously cited, p. 513.

30. Another variation is the one proposed over four hundred years ago in the Middleburg Liturgy of the English Puritans (1586). "Take and eate, this bread is the body of Christ that was broken for us. Doo this in remembrance of him" and "Drinke ye all of this: This cuppe is the newe Testament in the bloud of Christ, which was shedde for the sinnes of manie: Doo this in remembrance of him." Thompson, *Liturgies of the Western Church*, previously cited, p. 338.

31. "This is My Body," in *Essays on the Lord's Supper* by Oscar Cullmann and F.J. Leenhardt, translated by J.G. Davies [Ecumenical Studies in Worship I] (London: Lutterworth, 1958), p. 74.

32. *The Roman Missal. Sacramentary* (Huntington, IN: Our Sunday Visitor, 1974), p. 682.

33. Minister's Desk Edition (Minneapolis: Augsburg, 1978), p. 277 and elsewhere.

34. Commission on Worship of the United Methodist Church (Nashville: Methodist Publishing, 1981), no page numbers.

35. *Service Book for the Use of Ministers Conducting Public Worship* (Toronto: Ryerson, 1969), pp. 1–36.

36. (London: Hodder and Stoughton, 1980), p. 143.

37. *Ibid.*, pp. 197–198.

38. Manuscript copy, 5:40–41.

39. *Ibid.*, 6:15–16.

40. This essay was originally published in the *Anglican Theological Review.*

41. Pp. 338, 365.

42. "Three Languages of Christian Sacraments," *Worship* 52:574.

Chapter Six

On Liturgical Hospitality

Prologue

What shall I write to honor Frank Sugeno? The question arose. My original notion was to gather an interest of deep concern to Frank, namely, Christian mission, and one of deep concern to me, namely, liturgy, and to treat them together, as has been done before. The union of these ideas leads me to remember important work done some thirty years

ago by Massey Shepherd, an essay called "Liturgy and Mission" in a collection entitled, *Liturgy as Mission,* edited by Frank Stephen Cellier.[1] A re-reading of this essay alerted me to important changes that have occurred in the years which have passed between then and now, and suggested a different direction for these remarks.

Shepherd's concern, as that of his fellow essayists, was particularly to commend to the Church the importance of Holy Eucharist as a theological idea and its centrality for liturgical practice. Shepherd's assumption was that because eucharist and mission were intimately related, the restoration of eucharistic practice to the common life of the church would bring about a heightened sense of mission. This kind of logic lay at the heart of much of the liturgical awakening which has occurred in the church over the last few decades.

In most parts of the Episcopal Church, it is now common enough practice for the principal service on Sunday to be the celebration of Holy Eucharist, just as the Prayer Book imagines. (BCP, p.13) This increase in eucharistic practice has rested in some measure on the revision of liturgical texts and the enrichment of the church's store of liturgical music. Insofar as these new materials have enlivened the spirit of the church, one cannot but rejoice at the work done. At the same time, it would be difficult to defend a claim that the more frequent celebration of the eucharist has carried with it the expected heightening in sensitivity to mission, understood either as evangelism or service. That it has not, has alerted some to the inadequacy of equating the revision of liturgical texts with the liturgical renewal of the church.[2]

Having taken this path in my thinking, I decided it wisest not to engage "liturgy and mission" as Shepherd and others have done, but rather to exchange that conception for a near relative. The logic of this new pursuit, however, continues to reside in the person of Frank Sugeno. The contents of the new pursuit I have gathered under the broad title, "liturgical hospitality."

In January, 1982, I came to Austin to interview for the appointment which I now hold.[3] During that visit, I went to lunch with Frank Sugeno. We sat at a table in the window of the Driskill Bar and Grill, a part of the venerable Driskill Hotel. We ate a pleasing lunch and began, over that table, a friendship that has expressed itself on many other occasions over many other tables.

As a table companion and host, Frank embodies in a quiet, attentive way, a deep and sustaining generosity. He shares his attention, his insight, his bounty and his humility in abundant and proper proportion. Frank Sugeno is a person of uncommonly generous hospitality. I find something godly in that.

It is then this yoking of meals (or table fellowship) and hospitality that gives rise to the collection of topics and comments which follow. They intend to honor Frank in their derivation from his good example. The "meal" in question is the church's Holy Eucharist, and by extension the whole of its liturgical repertoire. The content of "hospitality" will vary, as the reader will discover.

Introduction

"Practice hospitality" says Paul in Romans 12:13, and so we have. The writer of Hebrews directs us further, "Do not neglect to show hospitality to strangers, for thereby some have entertained angels unawares" (Hebrews 13:2). As the Lutheran theologian Frank Senn observes, "the practice of hospitality has been demonstrated in the history of Christianity, from the three days of free room and board provided to the traveling prophets in the late first-century church manual known as *The Didache* to the overnight accommodations provided by the medieval monasteries."[4] And clearly the practice continues in places where homeless people are sheltered and fed, where church picnics characterize the summer in small towns, where doors are opened and people invited in, where strangers are welcomed.

What is of concern to us in these reflections is the relation of ideas of hospitality and the liturgical life of the church. The set of concerns to be explored is easily listed, though surely the list could be considerably longer. Of particular interest here are liturgical inculturation as derivative of the church's calling to hospitality, the public (and therefore hospitable) nature of Christian worship, the liturgical environment as a place of hospitality and some comments on the hosting of a community of hospitality. (It is perhaps evident to some readers as to how the current set of interests evolved from the initial concern with liturgy and mission.)

Liturgical Inculturation

The literature which treats the matter of liturgical inculturation typically contains citations bearing the name of Anscar Chupungco. For twenty years Chupungco, a Filipino Benedictine teaching at the Pontifical Institute in Rome, has helped many gain clarity on matters of liturgical adaptation. His writings have provided his readers with a very helpful set of categories for cultural/liturgical analysis.

In his most recent book, *Liturgical Inculturation: Sacramentals, Religiosity and Catechesis,* he reviews these categories.[5] Using a vocabulary generated from Roman Catholic circles, he distinguishes between indigenization, incarnation, contextualization, revision, adaptation, inculturation and acculturation. Each of these terms has had some measure of play in recent years, in and out of Roman Catholic circles. Of importance to us are the last two listed, inculturation and acculturation.

Taking them in the reverse order of consideration by Chupungco, acculturation is to be understood as the association of two cultures through external juxtaposition, the dynamic of interaction (mutual respect and tolerance) and the absence of mutual assimilation. Acculturation is, also, a precondition to inculturation. The author provides an equation for acculturation as follows: $A + B = AB$.[6]

Inculturation, on the other hand, involves a process of reciprocal assimilation between cultures, such that mutual influence is expected and prized. As to liturgical inculturation, and relying on official Roman Catholic sources, Chupungco recounts "the essential elements of inculturation, namely, the process of reciprocal assimilation between Christianity and culture and the resulting interior transformation of culture on the one hand and the rooting of Christianity in culture on the other."[7] He goes on to say, "Liturgical inculturation is basically the assimilation by the liturgy of local cultural patterns. It means that liturgy and culture share the same pattern of thinking, speaking, and expressing themselves through rites, symbols, and artistic forms. In short, the liturgy is inserted into the culture, history, and tradition of the people among whom the Church dwells. It begins to think, speak, and ritualize according to the local cultural pattern." Chupungco's equation here is $A + B = C$.[8]

As a strategy for the liturgical missionary, Chupungco's vision shows a generosity toward the "receiving" culture that certainly has not characterized efforts of earlier generations. The inherent value accorded to each of the players in the process of inculturation—the liturgy received and the culture of reception—makes possible a kind of reciprocity unique to more recent times. In theory, both the liturgy and the culture become hospitable to one another.

At the same time, this generosity, this expectation of hospitality, is anchored in the necessary role played by what the author calls "typical editions" of the liturgical texts themselves.[9] One gets the clear impression that although inculturation has a certain mutuality about it, the "typical editions" are in fact texts which are intended to survive intact the process of inculturation. It is here that we meet a factor of inhibition in our analysis of liturgical inculturation as an instance of liturgical hospitality.

There is about true hospitality a certain vulnerability that is finally not present in the mutuality of inculturation if, for example, the "typical editions" are, in fact, intended to survive engagement with culture. Instead of vulnerability, there is, instead, a withholding of possibilities, a protection of what is offered which denies the real possibility of innovation. Mutuality is thwarted thereby.

Turning now to a different source, one finds a somewhat more open, hospitable option, at least by my reading. Writing in the introduction to a collection of essays he edited, entitled *Liturgical Inculturation in the Anglican Communion*, Canadian David R. Holeton suggests an interpretation of inculturation that leaves true reciprocity more available.[10]

For years, Anglicans have said that the Book of Common Prayer served as the adhesive, the glue holding the Anglican Communion together. As more and more members of the Communion have developed liturgical texts which supplement and in some instances replace the authorized BCP texts, the question arises as to the dependability of the former wisdom. And beyond the holding of the Communion together, the liturgical evolution underway among Anglicans raises for some the question of Anglican identity itself.[11]

To this challenge, Holeton proposes the following observation: "The basic glue which holds us together as Anglicans is not the Book of Common Prayer nor even the spirit of the Prayer Book but, rather, our common will to live together as a communion of churches acting faithfully to proclaim the gospel among every people and culture."[12] This view opens, to the peril of some no doubt, a very wide vista for cultural influence in liturgical adaptation and creativity.

Holeton's introduction serves as a preface for "The York Statement, 'Down to Earth Worship,'" further titled, "Liturgical Inculturation and the Anglican Communion." In the York Statement, though properly cautious as one might expect, there is in evidence, nonetheless, a venturesome hospitality attractive to this writer. The statement reads in part, "We gladly acknowledge that true local cultural expression in worship has in some places gone far ahead of official provision. Sometimes this is to be found in the 'official' liturgy, sometimes outside of it; sometimes the desire to be untrammeled springs from the joy of charismatics or the fervour of the East African Revival, sometimes from more measured and careful introduction of truly local colour. In conformity with our main inculturation principles, we believe such ways should be welcomed, not wholly uncritically, but with a strong prejudice in their favour."[13]

In this statement, one gets a rather different sense of the meaning of inculturation. Whereas with Chupungco, one gets the sense that the task at hand in the situation of liturgical inculturation is for the received texts to exert or impress the tradition upon the receiving culture, such that the "past" is certainly the enduring reality. With Holeton and the York Statement, one senses the possibility that the "future" may also be a locus of authority, that the liturgical reality to emerge from the occasion of inculturation may be more "true" than what was initially received.[14]

Surely this latter is the more hospitable alternative, the more generous. And surely the more risky. Yet, if one were convinced that certainty, liturgical certainty as well as all other kinds, was the prerogative of God and not ourselves, then one could rest a bit more easily with the risk and dwell, instead, on the possibilities of receiving something from the future more rich and rewarding than what we have known to now. Frank Senn is surely right when he says, "The issue of inculturating the liturgy is really the question of authentic celebration and proclamation of the gospel."[15] The question is, where is "authenticity" to be found?

"Public" Worship

It is common enough among us to speak of the worship life of the church as "public." Yet to make this assertion carries with it some interesting implications. To speak of Christian worship as "public" is to assert both that it occurs in public and that it occurs amidst a public. This observation comes to us with special power through the work of several recent writers.

As to what "public" might mean in this or any context, we gain insight from Parker Palmer (*The Company of Strangers: Christians and the Renewal of America's Public Life*) and Patrick Keifert (*Welcoming the Stranger: A Public Theology of Worship and Evangelism*). Both rely in some measure on the observations of Richard Sennett (*The Fall of Public Man*).[16]

The besetting problem for all these writers is the withering of the patterns and protective structures of public life and their virtual replacement in our value system by patterns and assumptions rooted in a more private or intimate world. Instead of public (and corporate) norms serving us, they suggest that these norms have been replaced by standards or expectations rooted in the self or the individual. The great loss here is that public and corporate norms make space for the stranger. Private or individual norms typically do not. Hence, by using private or individual norms as if public or corporate, place for the stranger, in our common imagination, has been foreclosed. "In public," writes Palmer, "we remember that the world consists of more than self and family and friends."[17] Given the place in the biblical heritage given to "the stranger," the loss of such is a serious one. (One ought to add that "diversity" is also sacrificed when tested by typical "intimate" norms.)

The characteristics Palmer offers for "public life" (what a "public" does or what happens "in public") are quite illuminating: strangers meet on common ground; fear of strangers is faced and dealt with; scarce resources are shared and abundance is generated; conflict occurs and is resolved; life is given color, texture, drama, a festive air; people are drawn out of themselves; mutual responsibility becomes evident, and mutual aid possible; options become audible and accountable; vision is projected and projects are attempted; people are empowered and protected against power.[18]

The subversion of this set of possibilities has been accomplished by the imposition of "the norm of intimacy (which applies primarily to private life) upon the public sphere. For within the public realm, where most relations are necessarily distant and impersonal, the demand for closeness and warmth distorts and eventually destroys the potential of public experience." The "ideology of intimacy" has, as it were, captured our "public" imagination.[19]

Building on Palmer's premise, Patrick Keifert explores how this reading of "public" informs "public" worship. He is persuaded, as I am, that the "ideology of intimacy" has found expression in our liturgical life and that that expression, if left uncontested or without supplement, is not a particularly good thing. The typical symptom of this phenomenon is demonstrated in the expectation that the primary intent of the liturgy is that the individual "get something" out of it. In addition, our current fascination with the language of "family" and our rather too frequent burdensome use of this metaphor carry an obvious danger. This sort of imagery makes no place for the stranger, the figure whom Palmer calls the "key figure in public life."[20] Perhaps the real issue is the virtual singularity of this metaphor. What may be needed most is another metaphor as a complement, a companion of sorts.

In order to challenge the influence of intimacy as a determinative standard for life in public and for public worship, Keifert proffers the biblical image of hospitality to strangers. The "stranger" to whom Keifert addresses himself comes in three expressions: (1) the true "outsider," the one who is other; (2) the "inside" stranger, the member of the group who is marginal to the life of the group; and (3) the stranger which is the "irreducible difference which exists between two persons . . . in any encounter."[21] In an appropriate extension of the image, following Palmer, Keifert argues that the church itself would be very well served to understand itself as, in fact, "a company of strangers."[22]

It is here that we touch a powerful and neglected idea—the church as itself "a company of strangers." Instead of imagining ourselves as a company of intimates and generating a theology or a pattern of liturgical behavior on that assumption, what would our selfsense be if "the stranger" were a principal and evocative metaphor? Further, if we set this image center stage, it would require that we accept the fact that our being "strangers," one to another, is neither good nor bad. It is just so. "Hospitality means letting the stranger remain a stranger while offering acceptance nonetheless. It means honoring the fact that strangers already have a relationship—rooted in our common humanity—without having to build one on intimate interpersonal knowledge, without having to become friends."[23] And, taking this one step further, we Christians are strangers not only with a common humanity but also with a common life, a "public" life, grounded in the person of Jesus Christ. We are "strangers" gathered with him, open to the company of other "strangers," as earlier strangers were open to us.

Palmer writes, "We must learn to accept and appreciate the fact that public life is fundamentally impersonal. Relations in public are the relations of strangers who do not, and need not, know each other in depth."[24] Here is a genuine challenge to our current liturgical self-understanding. One need only attend certain parishes and observe the exchange of the peace to understand what a challenge this "public impersonality" really is. The formal, public, stylized action imagined by the "public" (corporate) liturgy is frequently exchanged for an action whose intimacy certainly exceeds ritual necessity. The stranger is either assaulted by some zealot or ignored in favor of some more preferred "neighbor." In either case, hospitality is neglected.

This being so, for life in public, for public worship, what character might our liturgical life have in order to be hospitable? Keifert answers, "Hospitality to the stranger implies wisdom, love, and justice—rather than intimacy, warmth, and familiarity—in our dealings with others in public."[25] Wisdom, love, justice. How these might be expressed in the liturgy would vary from time to time and place to place. The point is that in public, we would act in public ways, on public assumptions, guided by public (corporate) norms. In private, other norms, perhaps inclusive of the public ones, would be appropriate.

Liturgical Environment

To associate hospitality with a building is typically to make reference to the hospitality of the people who inhabit or use the space. But there is, also, it seems to me, a kind of hospitality that a built environment might itself possess or offer.

Perhaps the first necessity of hospitality for a building to possess is some degree of legibility. That is, the building must extend to the stranger (first time visitor) some invitation to enter, some notion of the vulnerability of welcome. One feels, for example, the acute absence of this vulnerability at the Episcopal Seminary of the Southwest. Our campus is explainable only historically. The Seminary buildings were built around a grand old house that dominates the block on which the Seminary sits. The uninformed might suspect that the "grand old house," called Rather House, contained the principal entry to the campus. Not so! Indeed, its use is so occasional that it ought rightly to be the last place to go to locate anyone. Indeed, truth be told, the Seminary campus really has no "front door," no point of identifiable access, no place that says, "Welcome." In that our campus, "our home" is indecipherable, it is inhospitable. In this sense, the visitor to our campus is treated inhospitably by the collection of buildings. So in our efforts at human hospitality, we begin with a deficit. Initially, then, this sense of welcome, of vulnerability is essential if a built environment is to be hospitable.

Writing about the time of Christ, the Roman architect, Vitruvius, distinguished three qualities typical of a built environment, *venustas* (beauty), *utilitas* (function), and *firmitas* (structure). These qualities are best known to English-speaking readers as delight, commodity and firmness, after Sir Henry Wotton.[26] For Vitruvius, the central matter of concern was *venustas;* for our purposes, it is commodity, the ability of an architectural space to accommodate what it is intended to shelter. Putting this in terms suitable to the current topics, the question is, is the environment hospitable to the work or activity for which it exists?

The liturgical environment exists, first of all, to shelter the gathered prayers of the community of the baptized—to shelter though not to contain them. For such a shelter to be commodious, one must know what "forms" the prayers will take, what patterns of movement and settledness must be housed, what receptivity must the environment possess in order to create a true "place."

It was questions like these that lay at the heart of work which preoccupied my sabbatical time several years ago. I sought to learn, from those who had designed relatively new liturgical spaces for the Episcopal Church, exactly how the rites of the church informed their sense of design. Sadly and strangely, my findings suggested to me that these questions were rarely or barely asked. Much, instead, was taken for granted about our liturgical tradition, to the neglect of the more abundant possibilities available to the church in the current Prayer Book.

Some illustrations. For a room to be hospitable to the baptismal assumptions contained in the Prayer Book, something other than a candy-dish on a pedestal is required for a font. Indeed, the rite imagines a rather more dangerous and powerful place, a pool, perhaps, large enough to drown in, large enough to be raised from. Recognition of this "fact" ought to prompt designers to conceive a design that would accommodate or "be hospitable to" such possibilities.

Further, if the environment is to be hospitable to the rites of the church, the designers of liturgical spaces ought to take with more seriousness the spatial implications of liturgical variety. The Prayer Book contains a remarkable array of images, theological ideas and textures. This variety has physical and spatial consequences which our liturgical environment needs to accommodate. I have argued elsewhere that a flexible liturgical environment is more fully expressive of the nature of our current liturgical life than a static one.[27] I have associated the varying of the environment with the seasons of the church year. This association would then lead me to test the hospitality of a liturgical environment by its hospitality to the richest expression of the church's corporate memory, that is, the calendar, our "remembrancer."

Beyond the hospitality of the space to the liturgical activity of the church, we must consider the relationship of hospitality and matters of justice and mercy. The most obvious instance of this relationship is what we commonly call "accessibility."

Churches have come rather late to this expression of hospitality. Indeed, if my own explorations are dependable, we have yet to see "access" as a theological notion, much less a matter of justice and mercy. God, however, being the devious one, we now have some measure of "justice and mercy" enshrined in law, in the form of the Americans with Disabilities Act (January, 1992). We can now no longer do otherwise. Our building must be gracious to us all.[28]

At the same time, and noting the general clericalization of the church's liturgy, it is ironic for me to report the following. During the sabbatical research to which I have previously referred, I visited 31 Episcopal church buildings, each built with some reference to the architectural assumptions present in the current revision of the Prayer Book. In each place, I inquired about "access," and in each instance the buildings were described as "accessible." I found this claim to be true as regards congregational aspects of the buildings, but false, with one exception, as regards the areas typically occupied by the priest. In only one building was the altar/table accessible by ramp.

One wonders, as well, as to how concerns for justice might influence the configuration of the liturgical assembly. Are there ways that we might order ourselves spatially which would more adequately and with more justice express our true selves? What shape or pattern most richly, most truthfully expresses our understanding of the Reign of God? I am not persuaded of a clear answer to this powerful question but I suspect that some configuration in which the first might be last and the last first would come close, a place where the table to which all were invited was not blocked by elevations and "fences," where leadership was signaled and exercised from "within" the community and not "apart" from it, high and lifted-up. Such a room might suggest that in it, justice was done and seen to be done, and mercy as well.

The Work of the Host

It remains now to consider some matters of liturgical hospitality to be associated peculiarly with the one who presides. In the semester during which this *Festschrift* is to be published, I intend to be on sabbatical leave, writing a book-length manuscript (I cannot bring myself to say "writing a book") which will include consideration of the presider as host. (The manuscript is currently titled, "Shaped by Images: The One who Presides.")[29] In that longer manuscript, I hope to explore a fairly wide array of topics, only one or two of which warrant treatment here.

For years, I have valued the culinary/theological work of Robert Capon. His *Supper of the Lamb* has been a frequent gift of mine to others and I have, myself, been the recipient of more than one of his other volumes treating matters of hospitality.

In his *Party Spirit,* the author invites us to consider "host" as an idea and as a kind of work or responsibility.[30] His observations are useful companions to things I want to say later. I should add that I set these observations alongside the comment of Patrick Keifert, who says, "God is the host of public worship," knowing that for some there may be in this combination of ideas an inherent contradiction.[31] I would only say that insofar as the liturgical assembly is seen to have a visible host, that host is the one who presides, perhaps as a sign, echo, mirror, souvenir, icon, reminiscence, instrument, or some such, of God's hospitable action. In any case, the presider's work as host and the assembly's responsibilities naturally exist in a symbiotic relationship.

Returning to Robert Capon, he suggests that the simplest meaning of "host," that of provider or shelterer, "sets forth the primary obligations of the party-giver: food sufficient, drink abundant and some better ground than a street corner on which to reckon with them."[32] Adding to this the image of "host" as an army, sallying forth, and, by extension, the "heavenly court of the Lord of Hosts himself," Capon goes on to say,

"The giver of a party . . . is called to more than mere provision. He must have within him not only the resoluteness of an earthly host but the accomplished joy of the heavenly one." [33]

To these initial dimensions, Capon adds even more rich ones, the scientific and the theological. The scientific meaning, of course, holds the notion that the host is fed upon and thereby sustains others; and the theological, closely related, that the host is "the offered victim of a sacrifice." He writes, " . . . the host unprepared to be drained personally as well as financially is a host simply unprepared . . . This seems extreme, I know. But on any but the most trivial view of a party, it is exactly right. The labor of love to which a host goes cannot be confined to the slicing and dicing he does in advance, nor even to the actual service of his guests when they arrive. What he really owes them as a result of his sovereign call to company is his undivided attention. And to them, not simply to their needs." [34]

Translating Capon's observations from the domestic to the liturgical setting is easy enough, though obviously the translation is not accomplished without remainder. And caution must be expressed about isolating the presider (as "host") from the assembly (as if "guests"). I do eagerly admit the mutuality which resides at the very heart of the work of the liturgy, but surely the same might be said for the finest of parties.

So, the host, the one who presides. For the purposes of this essay, two matters of liturgical hospitality are of particular moment, the one having to do with precedence and the other to do with decorum.

The eucharistic liturgy and its physical setting are filled with images and metaphors, some more powerful than others. Among the most powerful is the meal. It is common enough for us to speak of the eucharist as a meal and the altar as a table. Eucharist as meal, presider as host. This would be the logic. This being so, it seems odd to me, given our cultural assumptions about hosting a meal, that the rubrics say the following: "The ministers receive the Sacrament in both kinds, and then immediately deliver it to the people;" and "While the people are coming forward to receive Communion, the celebrant receives the Sacrament in both kinds. The bishops, priests, and deacons at the Holy Table then communicate, and after them the people" (BCP, 365, 407).

" . . . and after them the people." In what other social setting would the host eat first? I can think of none. Surely the norm is quite the opposite. Following on Capon's testimony, it seems obvious that the host's first responsibility would be to see that all in attendance ate and drank well, after which then the host (and others sharing that responsibility) might eat. The host would not eat first and then invite the others to join, but would rather first distribute the food with care to others in hopes that all would have ample portion. Then, when all were cared for, the host would be fed.

The rubrical directives in the Prayer Book remain consistent with the received tradition, a tradition seemingly rooted in hierarchical precedence rather than hospitality. Reading this precedence in a certain way, the rubrics seem to suggest that the communion is properly the priest's communion, into which the people are invited to share. By this reading, should the peoples' invitation to receive be taken as evidence of priestly "generosity?"

Among the Anglican liturgical books in current use, the restrictive nature of our Prayer Book is unusual in its consistent stipulation that the presider receive before the people. *The Alternative Services Book* (1980) in the Church of England and *The Book of Alternative Services* (1985) in the Anglican Church of Canada make no such rigid requirement, but, at least on some occasions and in certain rites, simply direct that the presider and people are to receive the Sacrament. Would that our revision were as liberal!

For my part, following the logic I have tried to lay out, I would write the rubric such that the presider (and those assisting in the distribution of the elements) receive after all have been fed. The sign value here would rest on the social conventions rightly attached to "the host" and to the fact that the serving role is at the heart of such work. The one ordained to preside, the one who is authorized to speak the Great Thanksgiving, the one who wears for the community the festal garment, this person is the servant who hosts the liturgy. Eating last would show this forth.

On this same issue Anscar Chupungco makes a useful observation, growing out of his own cultural setting in the Philippines. In order to explain why the *Misa ng Bayang Pilipino* (Mass of the Filipino People) directs that the priest take communion last, Chupungco says, "It is intended to express the Filipino concept and value of leadership and solicitude. To eat last is not only a sign of urbanity and social grace. Above all it represents service. Thus the host eats after the guests, because the host is expected to serve and move around. Parents take their meal after the children out of solicitude. At home a person forfeits or at least weakens his or her role as leader by taking food ahead of the others. In short, taking Communion last is, in the Filipino cultural context, an affirmation of the role of the priest as the president of the assembly."[35] This puts a different spin on the point under consideration here but comes to the same conclusion. Either as a sign of presidency or servanthood, eating last ought to be the hospitable norm.

The matter of decorum, to which we now turn, is dependent on the same eucharistic metaphor, the meal. As it seems proper for the host to eat after all have been cared for, so also it seems inhospitable for the host to consume all the "leftovers" while others merely watch. I try to imagine a dinner party in which, as the table was being cleared, the host (and a few helpers) ate what remained on the plates and drained the glasses of remaining wine, washed and wiped the dishes, all while the rest of us watched. Even with the addition of attractive music it seems a curious and inhospitable activity, almost rude.

The rubrics clearly invite the consumption of whatever remains of the consecrated elements after the Dismissal, that is, after the rite is over. Surely this is the better alternative. Do the dishes later! It is also worth noting that the ablutions are not peculiarly priestly work—"the celebrant or deacon, and other communicants, reverently eat and drink [whatever remains]" (BCP, 409)—even though the public, ceremonial doing of them would clearly suggest the opposite. The domestic practice is the best teacher here. Either do the dishes later or, as a happy alternative, invite *everyone* to help.

Further, consider the subtle social message contained in the action of the priest at the altar/table consuming the remains of the wine. Watching the priest stand at the altar/table and drink the remaining wine seems to dignify the abundant consumption of alcohol in an inappropriate way.

On Liturgical Hospitality

Certainly an addictive culture like ours does not need more such examples to fuel its dependencies.

In some places, the "space" in the liturgy created by the public doing of ablutions has attracted the attention of parish musicians, who have seen this as a time for special congregational or choir music. My suggestion of removing the ablutions to another time has elicited from some a mourning of the loss of that time for music. My response is to suggest that if the music is appropriate on its own terms, then it might be left there, with the presider going to sit where he or she belongs to enjoy it, or sing along, or do whatever is liturgically sensible.

The point is simply that doing the ablutions within the liturgy itself is not necessary and certainly not edifying. Nor is it hospitable.

On Liturgical Hospitality

It is perhaps appropriate in this "Decade of Evangelism" to explore the kinds of topics we have treated as a part of the consideration of mission strategy or something of the like. There is surely something to be said about the inherent attractiveness of hospitality, about the liturgy and the environment being attractive, hospitable, welcoming, evincing of justice and mercy, about the liturgical life of the church being "alluring." And by alluring I mean alluring such that the visitor, new person, potential "convert" finds a particular congregation or liturgical occasion inviting, a setting into which they might come again, a setting in which they might be willing to invest themselves, a setting in which they see and experience something of what is claimed in the words they hear spoken, the claims they hear made. But we must be careful with such a point of view, lest we inadvertently mislead ourselves.

What we intend by our hospitality is to show forth the graciousness of God. We do not intend to set a trap for the innocent. We are not intending to set bait. The justification for our hospitality is to be found in our imitation of the ministry of Jesus. To the extent that our "imitation" is authentic, faithful, aided by the Spirit, then to that same extent and for that reason alone, it will be "alluring."

I have said in class for years that there is no such thing as a pure motive, and so it surely is here as well. Yet, we must, as purely as possible, ground our liturgical hospitality in the example of our gracious Lord and not elsewhere, and for the sake of that example we must be willing to "succeed" in the task of evangelism as the Spirit sees fit. This is to say, our calling is to hospitality for Jesus' sake, and not for our own.

---

1. (New York: Seabury, 1964).

2. At the 1992 meeting of the Anglican/Episcopal members of the North American Academy of Liturgy, Paul Bradshaw delivered a paper on this topic.

3. The chair that I occupy is the J. Milton Richardson Chair in Liturgy and Anglican Studies. It is worth noting that Milton Richardson, while serving as the Bishop of Texas, refused to vote in favor of the current revision of the Book of Common Prayer. This fact caused one graduate of this Seminary to observe that being the J. Milton Richardson Professor of Liturgy was rather like being the George S. Patton Professor of Peace Studies.

4. *The Witness of the Worshiping Community* (New York: Paulist, 1993), p. 92.

5. (Collegeville, MN: The Liturgical Press/Pueblo, 1992), Chapter One.

6. *Ibid.*, p. 27.

7. *Ibid.*, p. 29.

8. *Ibid.*, p. 30.

9. *Ibid.*, p. 32.

10. Alcuin/GROW Liturgical Study 15 (Bramcote, Notts, UK: Grove, 1990).

11. See Paul Gibson's essay, "What is the future role of liturgy in Anglican unity?" in *Liturgical Inculturation in the Anglican Communion*, previously cited. This paper was first presented at a meeting of the Anglican/Episcopal members of the North American Academy of Liturgy.

12. "Introduction" in *Liturgical Inculturation in the Anglican Communion*, previously cited, p. 7.

13. "The York Statement" in *Liturgical Inculturation in the Anglican Communion*, previously cited, p. 13.

14. Frank Senn has some useful observations on this issue in his chapter called "Invitational Evangelism: Hospitality and Inculturation" in *The Witness of the Worshiping Community*, previously cited.

15. *Ibid.*, p. 102.

16. Palmer (New York: Crossroad, 1992); Keifert (Minneapolis, MN: Fortress, 1992); Sennett (New York: Random House, 1978).

17. Palmer, *The Company of Strangers*, previously cited, p. 35.

18. *Ibid.*, pp. 40–46.

19. This is Sennett's phrase, quoted by Palmer, *The Company of Strangers*, previously cited, p. 49.

20. *Ibid.*, p. 56.

21. Keifert, *Welcoming the Stranger*, previously cited, pp. 8–9.

22. *Ibid.*, p. 90.

23. Palmer, *The Company of Strangers*, previously cited, p. 68.

24. *Ibid.*, p. 50.

25. Keifert, *Welcoming the Stranger*, previously cited, p. 80.

26. See Spiro Kostof, *A History of Architecture: Settings and Rituals* (New York: Oxford, 1985), p. 13.

27. See my article, "An Apology for Variable Liturgical Space," in *Worship* 61/3 (May, 1987), pp. 231–242. [It is contained in the present volume.]

28. It is ironic to note, however, that, given the "separation" of Church and State, this legislation applies variously to churches. Morally, of course, we must be in compliance.

29. The book was actually written and published in 1995. The title was change from what was proposed here. The word "the" was left out.

30. *Party Spirit: Some Entertaining Principles* (New York: William Morrow, 1979).

31. Keifert, *Welcoming the Stranger*, previously cited, p. 58.

32. *Party Spirit*, previously cited, p. 24.

33. *Ibid.*

34. *Ibid.*, pp. 24–25.

35. Chupungco, *Liturgical Inculturation*, previously cited, p. 41.

Chapter Seven

De-coding the Obvious

*Reflections on Baptismal Ministry
in the Episcopal Church*

Stating the Problem

The Episcopal Church is re-awakening to the importance of Christian
initiation.[1] The texts in the Book of Common Prayer and *The Book of
Occasional Services* are the

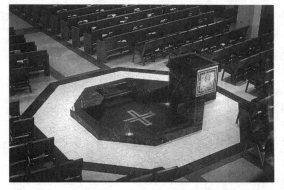

best signs and continuing
sources of this re-awakening. Clearly, the rites for
baptism and the series of
rites associated with the
catechumenate, combined
with the Prayer Book's directive regarding the public nature of initiation, the
naming of baptismal days and the heightened place given the Easter Vigil
in our ritual life, all work to enhance and invigorate the church's baptismal practice.

In addition to these texts and rubrical norms, there are meetings, conferences and books which augment and interpret the liturgical texts,
teaching and encouraging the church in its initiation practices. Among
these are Daniel Stevick's *Baptismal Moments; Baptismal Meanings* (1987),
The Baptismal Mystery and the Catechumenate, edited by Michael Mer-
riman (1989) and the 1991 revised edition of A. Theodore Eastman's *The
Baptizing Community* (1982). Further, in groups like the Associated Par-

ishes and the Association of Diocesan Liturgy and Music Commissions, the Episcopal Church has people of deep concern and insight offering their gifts in pointed and programmatic forms to any and all interested.

From these and many other quarters, both within and without the Episcopal Church, efforts mount to empower the rites which make Christians, to give a true place to the complex ritual act which bestows forgiveness of sins and raises to newness of life, which seals by the Spirit of God and makes one Christ's own forever. In the face of all this, one must first of all cheer about this turn of events, and having cheered, as surely I do, then to work to assist the enterprise.

It appears that the assistance I can offer is of a peculiar sort. That is, what I find myself able to do is to identify impediments to the process. In fact, I find myself convinced that the real and effectual power of Christian initiation in the Episcopal Church faces dismal prospects for true and faithful "success." This is so on two grounds, namely, spatial evidence and ritual evidence. What I intend in the following remarks is to examine this physical evidence with an eye to "de-coding the obvious."[2]

In a way, what I am suggesting is that what we claim about the importance of initiation is *not* supported by the physical, observable evidence. The failure to support discredits our claims. And if evangelism is to be central to the work we are about, then surely this rite of conversion and incorporation needs to be healthy and to tell the truth to those drawn into the fellowship of Christ.

Spatial Evidence

The central ritual metaphor underneath all the rites in the Prayer Book is an encounter, an encounter between the gathered community and God. This encounter is acted out and experienced in the church's public liturgy around three liturgical centers within a common liturgical space.

The ecclesiology of the Prayer Book sees the church as a community.[3] Liturgically speaking, the work of this community is distributed among the several members and enacted in the gathering. The clear supposition is that the community will all gather in the same room, rather than in several rooms, as in older architectural styles. (At its most extravagant, a Gothic building had three rooms—one for the baptized, one for the choir (clergy) and one for the ordained presider.)

In addition, because the liturgical work is distributed in a functional rather than hierarchical fashion, there is no need for the space to be hierarchically ordered, though clearly one must be sensitive to the needs of hearing and seeing. This way of viewing the space requires that we abandon the older names (nave, chancel, sanctuary) and search for new ones. Interestingly enough, so far as I can tell, the search has yet to yield a really usable vocabulary.

In addition to a single room, this view of the church requires a configuration that in a tangible way sets forth testimony to "gathering around." This leads to the abandonment of the linear, rectangular building (the one modeled on the bus) in favor of some configuration several-sided around the central focus. This notion tends to create a room that is wider than it is deep. A circular configuration has attracted some, though under most circumstances I would argue against the circle on both practical and theological grounds.[4]

If a single chamber is most congruent with the intent of the Prayer Book, the inter-relationship of the liturgical centers within that space is our next concern. The three centers are the place for baptism, the place for liturgy of the word and the place for the liturgy at the altar/table. In Marion Hatchett's occasional paper, "The Architectural Implications of the Book of Common Prayer 1979," he says that these three liturgical centers "should have approximately equal dignity and prominence."[5]

My own way of expressing this is to view the liturgical space as if it were an ecosystem, an interactive community of organisms within an environment. This way of understanding the existence and organization of space puts the *inter-relationship* of these centers on equal footing with their own particular and individual integrity. A sound ecosystem is dependent on mutual necessity and reciprocity. Consequently, as a metaphor for the character of a liturgical space, an ecosystem establishes *balance* as a central characteristic.

The ambo and altar/table constitute two of the three liturgical centers which populate our liturgical environment. The baptismal space is the third, and the principal concern of this essay.

Surely there is no subject in liturgical studies more warmly or richly treated in our time than baptismal rites and theology. Human concern for identity, membership and initiation coupled with ever greater curiosity about the activity of God's Holy Spirit have brought out of us more and more powerful convictions about this rite of burial, birth and bathing.

"Holy Baptism is full initiation by water and the Holy Spirit into Christ's Body the Church. The bond which God establishes in baptism is indissoluble."[6] So reads the Prayer Book. Although debates still arise throughout the church as to what confirmation is, the importance and centrality of the water rite are not in dispute. Consequently, and in principle at least, there is also no debate about the importance of the ritual object which must bear the symbolic weight of our initiation theology. The rubrics imagine a place, a container, a pool of such size as to make possible the immersion of an adult.

Efforts in evidence in the Prayer Book to restore baptism to its rightful place and to give substance and symbolic power to the ritual object necessary for baptism have been fostered in large measure by a deeply held conviction about the calling of the baptized and the theological centrality of baptism. Theodore Eastman has spoken for many in saying, "baptism is ordination to the principal order of ministry."[7] In an important new book, *Anglicanism and the Christian Church,* Paul Avis calls baptism "the fundamental sacrament of Christianity" and "the ground of our unity." Further, he proposes a *"baptismal paradigm"* as the starting point for the church's own self-understanding and for conversations with other Christians.[8] Put another way, this suggests that the faith of "the blessed company of all faithful people" should be our primary place to stand rather than to require exclusively the company of "the successors of the apostles." This would provide us an ecclesiology formed on baptism, not ordination.

The foregoing suggests that at one level the Episcopal Church's teaching about baptism works to give the rite power, centrality, authenticity.

In practice, however, and in powerfully subtle ways, the current state of the physical evidence among us puts the lie to what we say.

In the spring and summer of 1990, with the aid of the Episcopal Church's Board for Theological Education, the Conant Fund and the Episcopal Theological Seminary of the Southwest, I completed a six-month sabbatical leave. The time was spent exploring the state of contemporary liturgical architecture in the Episcopal Church. To put it minimally, I was looking to see what we are building for ourselves, and in some way assessing the current work against the architectural and liturgical assumptions of the Prayer Book.

I made formal visits to 31 congregations across the United States.[9] Of the total, nineteen buildings had been built or reordered since 1980. In each visit I observed and photographed the liturgical space and made a drawing of the floor plan. In addition, by means of questionnaires designed for the purpose, I gathered information from the rector/vicar, musicians, members of the congregation and the architect/designer as to how the space "works."

With specific regard to the place for baptism (and based on this sample of 31 places), line drawings would suggest that typically fonts were placed either near entrances, on a main aisle, in their own niche or in the "east" end near the altar/table and ambo. These characteristics, alone or in combination, suggest that these fonts were in "correct" places. At the same time, of the places visited, four had no font in evidence. Of these four, two had small tables available on which bowls were placed when needed.

Only one of the sites visited would suggest to the observer that this room for proclamation and table-fellowship is also a room for baptism. The ritual object in this particular liturgical space would (almost) bear the theological weight our teaching would place upon it and would (almost) allow to happen what the rubrics presuppose. In virtually no other instance, perhaps with one exception, did the Prayer Book's renewed emphasis on baptism stimulate a more powerful spatial expression of our baptismal theology. Typically, I found small stone or wooden fonts, sometimes covered, sometimes not, sometimes containing a "candy dish,"

De-coding the Obvious

sometimes not, typically empty of water. Occasionally, it was clear to the observer that the most frequent role played by the font, particularly those near entrances, was as a place to set things, e.g., service leaflets.

During this tour across the country and the church, I was reminded again and again how powerful a symbol the altar/table is (often protected by rails, elevated spatially, adorned with special "clothing," typically approached and touched only by certain people, characterized by physical stability and permanence) and how subject to disregard the font (hidden away or absent, minimal in size, empty, trivialized in use). I was reminded again and again that ordained people attend the altar/table and that the (typically) incidental font is allegedly the place of empowerment of the baptized. I was thereby taught that the theological claims made for baptism were seriously challenged, even undermined by the subtle and persistent disjuncture between our claims and the physical evidence.

Ritual Evidence

If the spatial evidence signals an impediment to the success of our theological claims about the importance of baptism and the centrality to the Episcopal Church of the ministry of the baptized, the second stumbling block, in my view, is the difficulty created for our baptismal theology by a comparison of the baptismal rite and ordination. It is my opinion that claims about the empowerment for ministry associated with baptism will likely never find full expression so long as the rite of baptism is overshadowed by the rite of ordination. And ordination language in association with baptism will, frankly, only make things worse.

In order to make this point more clear, a "tour" of these two rites, baptism and ordination, seems appropriate. (Given my life's work in a seminary, I probably attend more ordinations than most people, certainly more than the typical parishioner, and likely more than is good for me. At the same time, the experience does give me a particularly good place from which to observe.) The following descriptions will necessarily lead to comparison.

Both of these are rites of passage, rites which are typically composed of three particular parts. The first part accomplishes the *separation* of the person(s) from their former status in the community; the second part accomplishes the *transition,* the passage intended; and the third part accomplishes the *reintegration* of the person(s) into the community. The transition phase is when "something happens," as it were. It is the most dynamic in ritual terms, the densest in meaning and, consequently, the most significant for our consideration. We shall therefore examine in turn the transition phase of the rites for baptism and presbyteral ordination as contained in the Book of Common Prayer.

In the baptismal liturgy, the transition phase begins with the movement of the baptismal party to the font if they are not there already. Here the water is poured if it has not been already and the water is blessed. The prayer formula begins in a way reminiscent of the Great Thanksgiving in the eucharist. "The Lord be with you. /And also with you." "Let us give thanks to the Lord our God. /It is right to give him thanks and praise." Following a reiteration of the role water plays in salvation history, the one who presides invokes the activity of God's Holy Spirit to sanctify this water. The rite assumes at this point that there is more than one candidate so the rubrics direct that each receive the water in turn. The "watering" then follows. After all have received the action of the water, the presider "in full sight of the congregation" prays for the sustaining power of the Holy Spirit and signs the forehead of each with a cross (and perhaps oil). Supplementary rubrics say the newly baptized may be given a candle. This is obviously not central. They are then welcomed by the assembly and thus reintegrated into the community. The peace of the Lord is exchanged as the newly baptized return to their seats in the assembly. The fact that the newly baptized have completed their transition (the passage) is fully expressed later in the rite by their admission to the fellowship of the altar/table.

We should notice that this rite is appropriately administered within the Sunday eucharist and especially appropriate on five occasions mentioned in the supplementary rubrics at the end of the rite[10] Also, although the bishop is (historically) the normative presider, in practice it is typically a presbyter who presides.

Turning now to the rite for the ordination of presbyter, we engage it at the comparable ritual moment, the moment of transition. All present are directed to stand, except the candidate who must kneel before the bishop, the necessary presider. The candidate is joined left and right by other presbyters. The clear supposition here is that there is just one candidate. (The supplemental rubrics printed at the end of the ordinal allow the possibility of more than one but this is obviously exceptional.) A hymn calling upon the Spirit is sung followed by a prescribed silence. The bishop offers a prayer of thanks after which he or she places both hands on the head of the candidate. The presbyters also lay on hands. The bishop then prays that God will fill the candidate with grace and power through the gift of the Spirit. Removing all the hands, the bishop continues in prayer petitioning God on behalf of the newly ordained. Following this prayer, the people are directed to respond "Amen" in a loud voice. The newly ordained is given appropriate vesture and the Bible, this latter as a sign of authority. The transition now accomplished, the process of reintegration is begun by the bishop greeting the newly ordained, who in turn extends the peace of the Lord to the assembly. The attending presbyters are directed by rubric to greet the newly ordained.

I hope I have described these rites so that their content and movement are clear. In each case, what I have described is part of a larger ritual event and each transitional phase is followed by the liturgy of Holy Communion. The differences between these rites are remarkable.

Presbyteral ordinations are typically understood to be preceded by an extended period of preparation (seminary), parochial sponsorship, testing and assessment (Commissions on Ministry and the General Ordination Exams) and an apprenticeship (diaconate). Baptisms are typically not.

Ordinations take place in public at special times, attendance by invitation. Baptisms take place in public but typically within the conventional Sunday liturgy. Invitations are not customary. Ordinations are usually attended by clergy who are vested, enter in procession and sit in a prominent place in the assembly. This is not typical of baptisms. Or-dinations are rites reserved to bishops, the chief liturgical officer. Baptisms may be but in practice usually are not. The rite of presbyteral ordination assumes only one candidate. Baptism presupposes more than one candidate. Ordinations are frequently filled with special music and festive ornaments. This is less so with baptisms.

The entrance rite for an ordination is built around the person of the ordinand, who has entered the room in procession accompanied by sponsors. The entrance rite for baptism is special to the occasion but is not built around the candidates, who typically have entered with the congregation and have not been a part of the entrance procession.

The readings for ordinations are specifically chosen for that rite and occasion, whereas the typical readings for baptism are the proper readings assigned to the Sunday liturgy. The preacher at an ordination is usually invited with great care and feeling by the ordinand. This is usually not the case at baptisms. In ordination sermons, there is typically a charge directed toward the ordinand. This is not so common at baptisms.

Ordinations take place at the "east" end of the liturgical space, the "front" so to say, towards which all the seats face and where the lighting and acoustics are generally good. In the "conventional" Episcopal Church, baptisms occur in the back of the room, at the west end, behind the assembly, "off-center," where lighting is often not sufficient and acoustics are often poor.

In the ordination rite, the moment of transition is accomplished with great force, signaled by the heading atop the page, "The Consecration of the Priest."[11] After the hymn invoking the Spirit a corporate silence is kept. Following a necessary silence, the candidate is surrounded or "buried" as it were in a heavy layer of hands, presbyteral as well as episcopal hands. Hands are the agents here of the sacrament. In contrast, at the transitional moment in conventional baptismal practice, titled "The Baptism," a minimal amount of sacramental "stuff" is used (that is a few drops of water) and it is typically dried off almost immediately lest anyone get wet!

De-coding the Obvious

Finally, whereas the newly baptized return to their seats in the assembly, where they were seated before, the newly ordained is invited "to take a higher seat," in proximity to the altar/table. In this way, the change of status is demonstrated.

Where does this comparison lead? To what conclusion do we come? In the narrow view, it seems that the ritual power of the ordination rite exceeds in practice that of baptism. At no step in our comparison does the action of baptism (as conventionally practiced) speak more loudly than ordination at a comparable point. Indeed, the ritual patterns upon which ordinations are built appear to be a combination of the wedding rite and a coronation. Baptism, on the other hand, has only its own self as its pattern, its being already a rite of incorporation. Certainly, the "spectacle" of the two is quite different.

It may seem harsh to say it, but on the basis of this comparison, what we want to claim about baptism and "the principal order of ministry" is ritual nonsense. And so long as that remains true, our teaching, however wise and faithful, however substantive and compelling, will be defeated by our ritual actions, which by this test contradict our theology.

Conclusions

In its simplest terms, I have suggested and (I believe) demonstrated that, in the Episcopal Church context, the truth told by our baptismal rite and the teachings we offer about it are *not* supported by our spatial and ritual evidence. Until such time as they are, we ought not to anticipate the real empowerment for ministry of the baptized. [In addition, we ought to anticipate the criticism from some quarter that "we" (clergy, perhaps) are really perfectly happy about that.] In the face of this evidence, it is surely a sign of God's benevolence to the church that the ministry of the baptized is as powerful as it is.

Behind this conclusion lies a particular theoretical perspective which has provided the methodology for this exploration. This perspective has two dimensions—ritual congruence and ritual coherence.

"Ritual congruence" signals the integrity, health, veracity of any particular ritual event; its absence signals the opposite. We come to congruence by analyzing the relationship of four aspects of any liturgical event. Firstly, there are obviously the *texts* themselves, the scripts, so to say. Insofar as the Book of Common Prayer is concerned, this would include not only the ritual text but also the rubrical material as well. Secondly, there is the *ritual action,* the work of the ritual community, which accompanies, animates and accomplishes the texts. Thirdly, there is the *environment* within which the action takes place, the setting, the things used. Lastly, all these exist and operate within a kind of *interpretive framework,* a theological understanding, a hermeneutic, as it were, which is admittedly and necessarily historically conditioned and contextual. In its healthier moments, the history of the church's liturgical tradition is marked by a high degree of ritual congruence among these four. In times of ill health, the absence of congruence has typically and eventually led to reform.

"Ritual congruence" then is a term aimed at the internal integrity of a rite, the ability of a ritual event "to tell the truth." I have suggested above that by this test, the baptismal liturgy of the Episcopal Church is not "congruent."

In addition to internal congruence, however, there is yet another point of assessment, namely, the correlation between a given rite and other rites in the complex. This second point of assessment is "ritual coherence." Beyond the initial question of the internal integrity of a rite, one must also examine the comparative claims made by various rites, and on this second basis as well, to render judgment. An analogy here might be found in ecumenical conversation. What Anglicans say in dialogue with Lutherans, for example, must have its own internal sense ("congruence"), and it must also make sense when put alongside what we say to Roman Catholics and the Orthodox ("coherence"). I have suggested above that when the rites of baptism and presbyteral ordination are compared with each other, ritual coherence is not achieved.

I am persuaded, along with many others, that the ritual life of a community is formative of that community. For us, that means that the liturgy is formative of the church. In the liturgy, in the midst of our praise of God, we remember and act out our identity. We describe to ourselves who we are, what we intend and hope for. It is on this basis that the *absence* of congruence and coherence regarding the baptismal liturgy has its subtle and unremitting impact on the self-understanding of the Episcopal Church.

Access to resolution of this problem is easier in spatial terms than in ritual terms. Such spaces would be proximate to the assembly, near a major entry, either visually accessible from congregational seating or located in an open area large enough for many of the congregation to gather about the font. The font itself would be of considerable size, preferably a pool in the ground though a raised font might also serve. In each case, water would be present, ideally flowing ("living") water. The location of the font and the presence of the water would invite those who enter to encounter again the water of baptism, and if given to such things, to make again the sign of the cross.[12]

Resolving the ritual problem is more difficult, since the conventional methods of liturgical reform and revision are rooted in the gradual evolution of rites, tested primarily by historical norms. What appears to me to be necessary is something quite different. First, we need to take seriously Paul Avis's tantalizing suggestion, mentioned earlier, that we fix our ecclesiology to a "baptismal paradigm." Commitment to such a paradigm would force us to talk more clearly about ministry in baptismal terms (as we struggle to do now) and then require us to ask the following ritual question: What would an ordination rite look/feel like that saw itself as dependent upon and derivative from the baptismal rite? In other words, what would an ordination rite look like that, as a by-product of its main intention, taught that the principal order of ministry in the church was brought into being elsewhere? What a revolutionary notion! It might be very interesting to see.[13]

Epilogue

The coherence question, inclusive as it is of multiple rites, must remain to another time to explore beyond the tantalizing suggestion made above. The matter of congruence, however, needs our attention, since the pursuit of this question could have direct consequences on the life and spirit of congregations, even without the further revision of texts.

If a congregation were to address itself to the question of congruence in its baptismal practice, given the rite(s) we now possess, how might this be done? Assuming certain conventions, common to Episcopal church buildings of a typical sort, there are certain considerations, which, if explored, would bring into greater alignment what we do and what we say.

At the outset, we should remember that "congruence" is to be understood as the happy relationship of four ingredients: texts (including rubrical material), ritual action, environment and the interpretive framework in which they reside. Since the liturgy itself is our great teacher and its cumulative power is formative of the church, a congregation seeking congruence is best advised to make careful assessment of its own lived-out experience on these four points. Deliberate truth seeking of this sort will lead to suggestions for greater congruence. (This kind of review might most profitably be done by an educated parish liturgy committee.)

For education in the pursuit of this assessment, the primary source is obviously the Prayer Book itself, but Theodore Eastman's book *The Baptizing Community* is a very useful companion. Reading the Prayer Book rites is the necessary first step.

What naturally follows, then, is a set of questions and concerns which could inform such an assessment. Consideration of these kinds of questions will help to clarify the parish's current practice and to give direction for change as needed.

First, as to textual considerations, this would necessarily involve a thorough review of the initiation rites in the Prayer Book, seeking to explore what the rites intend and provide. Careful attention would need to be given to both the rubrical directions and particularly to the theological content of the rite. In assessing the textual materials, it is likely that some measure of new awareness will begin to develop in those charged with the assessment. Study of the texts themselves often proves illuminating. For example, the careful reader will discover that whereas in the experience of most congregations, the normal (meaning the most commonly observed) baptismal candidate is an infant, the rite itself clearly assumes someone able to speak for themselves (an adult?) as the *normative* candidate, that is, the candidate the rite "has in mind." This same careful reader will also discover a richness of theological language and images still not clearly visible in the lived-out experience of baptized communities.

Secondly, consideration would need to be given to the ritual practice of the parish. How is the action of baptism accomplished? Are the baptismal days, as encouraged in the Prayer Book, followed in the parish? Are "private" baptisms done and under what circumstances? What value does water have in the parish's ritual bathing? (This seems a foolish question but the answer can be quite illuminating, given that water is the operative symbol in the rite.) How does the baptismal party enter the celebration (remembering that at ordinations, for example, the recipient of the sacramental action is a participant in the entrance procession, along with presenters/sponsors)? Do the sponsors do what the liturgy invites? On the baptismal days, in congregations in which multiple Sunday services is the norm, are baptisms celebrated at each or no? Or is there one central celebration at which the "whole" congregation is present? All these questions intend to invite an exploration of what actually goes on in the congregation's current practice of Christian initiation.

Thirdly, the liturgical environment for baptism would need analysis. Since most Episcopal churches do not have fonts that would allow immersion, even of infants, the question arises as to how to make a modest pedestal font as fitting a symbol as possible of the remarkable power of baptismal washing. Is the font a constant presence in the liturgical space or does it "appear" on certain festivals? Where is it placed, by an entry or somewhere else? Is it placed so that people "encounter" it during the course of the liturgy, or even on a non-liturgical visit to the space? Is the font approachable and welcoming, or separated and enclosed, perhaps with rails and suchlike? If the font has a cover, is it typically left on or left off the font? Is water kept continuously in the font, such that parishioners and any visitor might have the opportunity to engage the water on entering and leaving the space? (Many people, given the opportunity, will take the water upon their hand and make the sign of the cross, a regular and tactile kind of remembrance of one's own baptism.)

Another issue related to the liturgical environment is the nature of the lighting associated with the font. Is the font and the baptismal area lighted sufficiently and does the degree of illumination testify to the mutuality of altar/table, ambo and font? Further, what is the nature of the vesture and other ornaments associated with the parish's baptismal practice? Is sufficient dignity accorded to the baptismal rite by this means? (In considering this particular question, one ought to remember that the font itself and the water it contains are powerful and primary symbols. The use of symbols upon symbols, therefore, must be evaluated with great care. Simple, eloquent elements speak their own power.)

Finally, as to the environment, care needs to be taken as to how the font and its associated area are treated when not in ritual use. Put bluntly, is the edge of the font used as a place where things (leaflets, etc.) are "stored" as if on an end table? Is the area surrounding the font treated with proper dignity or is it frequently filled with folding chairs, for example, awaiting later use? (Though surely the common possession of the church, the font should not be treated as if a "common" object.)

Turning now to the fourth element in achieving congruence—the interpretive framework—several issues warrant attention. Perhaps the most important matter to explore is the nature of preaching and teaching in the parish about baptism and its place in the life of the church. What is the proclamation on baptismal days? Beyond this issue, what is the character, content and duration of catechesis in the parish for those preparing for baptism and/or sponsorship? Is the sponsorship of baptismal candidates an identifiable ministry in the parish? Does catechesis continue after baptism? Are the claims made in the parish about the nature of baptism and the ministry of the baptized acted out by clergy and laity alike? Does the parish understand itself as a "baptizing community"?

Another matter, smaller in proportion but telling nonetheless, is the question of the preparation of the parish congregation itself for baptismal occasions. Each time the church baptizes, the church experiences a change in itself. Is the congregation, in preparation for this baptismal change, given occasion to prepare itself to receive new members? Is notice given in advance of the baptismal days, declaring that on a day forthcoming, the congregation will witness death and resurrection, rebirth and initiation?

This set of issues and questions constitutes only suggestions as to how a particular parish might pursue congruence in its own practice of Christian initiation. My hope is that the results of such exploration might issue in a liturgical congruence that would give bold testimony to the place of baptism in the life of the Episcopal Church. Whether by this means or some other, there is surely ample reason to ponder the reality of our parochial (or diocesan) initiatory practice, with an eye to its enrichment. This is, after all, the Decade of Evangelism, a time dedicated to the making of new Christians and the upbuilding of the life of the church, a time begging for a remembered and lived-out liturgical theology which truthfully "decodes the obvious," thereby acknowledging this rite of burial, birth and bath as the centerpiece and organizing principle of ministry for all faithful people.[14]

---

1. Some of these ideas formed a part of one of the Rossiter Lectures I delivered at Bexley Hall, Rochester, N.Y., in the fall of 1988. I express my thanks to the Dean and Board for that invitation.

2. I am borrowing here the language of my friend and colleague, Charles James Cook.

3. See the Book of Common Prayer 1979, p. 854.

4. For those interested in this, see my article "An Apology for Variable Liturgical Space," in *Worship* 61/3 (May, 1987), pp. 240–241. (It is contained in the present volume.)

5. *The Occasional Papers of the Standing Liturgical Commission*, Collection Number One (New York: Standing Liturgical Commission, 1984), p. 1.

6. The Book of Common Prayer 1979, p. 298.

7. *The Baptizing Community* (New York: Seabury, revised 1991), p. 35.

8. (Minneapolis: Fortress, 1989), pp. 303–304.

9. Sites were visited in California, Illinois, Minnesota, Washington, Texas, Oregon, Missouri, Virginia and the District of Columbia.

10. These are the Easter Vigil, the Day of Pentecost, All Saints' Day or the Sunday following, the Feast of the Baptism of Jesus and on the occasion of the Bishop's visitation. The Book of Common Prayer 1979, p. 312.

11. The Book of Common Prayer 1979, p. 533.

12. I have seen good examples of the sort of space I describe here in several Roman Catholic churches. For example, St. John the Evangelist, Hopkins, MN; the Chapel of the Incarnation at the University of Dallas, Dallas, TX; and the Church of St. Francis of Assisi, Concord, CA. Among Episcopal churches that I know, I would cite the baptismal area at Grace Cathedral, San Francisco, and St. Matthew's Church, Pacific Palisades, CA.

13. I know of efforts in this direction in the Episcopal Diocese of Northern Michigan in which Bishop Thomas Ray has sought to associate baptism and ordination in the same ritual event. The texts used are obviously those from the Book of Common Prayer.

14. Many of the insights in this final section were contributed by my friend and former student, Amy Donohue.

Part Three

Moving
The
Furniture

Chapter Eight

An Apology for
Variable Liturgical Space

"The movement of the people, their changing position, the variation of the lighting, the solemn rhythms of the area of sound—all these together render that process which is the liturgy. It would be only a final step to give up the fixed structural space entirely and to use the structure simply as a means with which to render, in free creation, the ever-

changing space."[1] The extravagant imagination of Rudolf Schwarz invites another look at the use of liturgical space and its variation. Although surely not seeking to explore, much less describe "the cathedral of all times" (Schwarz's term), we do propose a new point of entry into a topic with some history.

Among those who see any virtue to variable liturgical space, and this is not necessarily a large group, the counsel to flexibility has been based either on a desire to avoid tying "knots in the future"[2] or on the recognition of a need for a multi-purpose space, an area intended to accommodate liturgical as well as other types of activities. Although quite sympathetic to both of these issues, and willing to argue each on its own terms, the current business is something rather different. Our concern is with the possibility of choosing and designing a flexible liturgical space, a variable liturgical environment, on liturgical or theological grounds.[3]

A disciplined exploration of this issue has been hovering on my horizon for some time. I was long ago intrigued by the views of J. G. Davies and the efforts of Davies and his cohorts at the Institute for the Study of Worship and Religious Architecture (Birmingham University) regarding multipurpose churches.[4] Even though I find myself less sanguine about them now than some years ago, I nonetheless have latched onto the notion of moving liturgical furniture and count it a happy possibility.

This interest in mobility has expressed itself from time to time in various ways. One example will serve. In November, 1985, the Architectural Commission of the (Episcopal) Diocese of Texas held a conference for the Diocese. Called "Architecture for Worship," and with apologies to Edward Sovik, the conference was intended for parishes at some stage in the process of imagining new or re-ordered liturgical spaces. Through the day-and-a-half conference, four liturgical events occurred (Morning Prayer, Vespers, Holy Eucharist, Noonday Prayers) along with lectures, panels, and discussions. The liturgical planners decided that it was important that each of the liturgies be in its own physical configuration, the room available having all the necessary furniture but nothing fixed to the floor or wall. The planners reasoned that the variety would enrich the experience and likely spark the imagination of the conferees, not to mention giving power to the liturgy itself. By all counts, the planners were right. This and other such experiences have made me curious about what there might be to this notion of variable space, below the surface, as it were.

Lastly, and in league with others, I admit to being quite persuaded that the liturgy is formative of the church[5] and with Frank Kacmarcik that "we are formed or deformed by the art and environment we experience around us."[6] This conviction about the formative role of the liturgy is fundamental to what follows.

The combination of a penchant for moving furniture and the sense that liturgy is formative, these I take to give permission for what follows. There are other preliminary or precautionary matters which might follow here but they will surface in due course.

An Apology for Variable Liturgical Space

Rationale

The rationale for a variable liturgical space can be provided quickly. It is exactly that for the varying of color, ornament, lections. What John Baldovin says (minimally) for ritual serves also (minimally) for spatial modulation. "Modulation in ritual, like modulation in color and decoration, is a non-verbal way of alerting people to the particular character of the liturgical celebration."[7] I say "minimally" because more than mere "alerting" goes on in this ordered variety.

The center of the church's ritual life is Jesus, through whom we know God and in whom we are known by God. It is the interchange or dialogue between knowing and being known which is modulated in the liturgy, Christ being the medium and the context. Our cycle of liturgical occasions invites us into the richness of this dialogue, as many-faceted and many-voiced as it is. Though chaos would cloud this richness and finally be destructive, ordered spatial variety exposes it more fully, enables entry and participation more completely.

This participation, in turn, acts itself out on us. We are taken by the ritual and made, perhaps made new, re-created. And each time re-creation occurs, the church is formed again, in this new occasion.

Basic to this activity, of course, is the keeping of the liturgical calendar, our ecclesial remembrancer and the narrator of our identity. One particularly happy freedom given the liturgical assembly by the seasons and the calendar is the freedom to say and do many things over a period of time. That is, because we know the calendar will take us where we ought to go, we need not be compelled either to do everything every time or to do the same thing each time. In a way then, the keeping of the calendar allows the tensions or dialectics in our faith, and in our liturgical life, to be expressed with integrity and not have to be disposed of in some too-easy accommodation.

We shall return to these points later on. For the moment it is sufficient to say that the possibility of varying the liturgical space is broadly related to the other variables in our liturgical life and finds its rationale there.

127

The proposed spatial "modulation," to use Baldovin's word, would intend the edification (upbuilding) of the assembly by providing a variable (and perhaps new) "point of view," "prospect," "place to stand."

Norms and Motifs

Having suggested that there is an existing rationale for the proposal at hand, the next question to arise is this: How to do this variation? If one were persuaded that spatial variety had some integrity on the face of it, what norms would be used for its implementation, what would be its rhythm or pattern? We shall move toward some suggestions.

Theologians debate with historians of religions about the character and necessity of holy places. We need take cognizance of this debate only to assert the following: (a) God's freedom to meet humankind wherever God pleases seems indisputable. And this everlasting possibility is surely consecratory of all creation. (b) At the same time, human beings require specificity. As Monica Hellwig has said, " . . . we cannot begin everywhere at once to discover holy ground. As with time in our lives, so is it with places. We have to begin by setting something apart. We have to respond to the outreach of God to us by co-creating with God special moments and places of encounter and communion with the divine presence and power."[8] The gathering of the liturgical assembly is such a time and place.

Thus, our discussion here is not about the idea "holy place" in a cosmic field. We take the existence of such places to be the consequence, the by-product of encounter and to be geographically located with the gathering, wherever two or three gather. Rather, our discussion is about the internal spatial character of structures intended to be these places of encounter with God. Here, you see, we admit that in the ritual activity done in such places, which are made holy places in the doing, the liturgical assembly *expresses* its nature and best self-understanding and, at the same time, *impresses* the same back upon itself. In so doing and in such spaces, the church as liturgical community is formed.

This being so, we turn to the matter of norms. Clearly whatever patterns were to be chosen, they would have to meet the same general standards established and operative for good liturgy. These standards would include (1) a single chamber for the assembly and the liturgical action; (2) a relationship between liturgical foci and people which encourages participation in the liturgical action and gives a sense of unity; (3) the liturgy of the word and the liturgy of the table should be clearly related and integrated; (4) the furniture which serve as foci for the liturgical action should be spatially related in significant ways.[9]

This list could be supplemented in various ways but the point is that whatever serve as the fundamental norms for contemporary liturgy must apply in each case. (To say this clearly carries with it the conviction that various spatial organizations will satisfy these basic standards.) A second set of norms (or really assumptions) must treat of things practical. For example, the obvious supposition in this essay is that the imagined liturgical environment is flexible, that none of the liturgical foci (altar/table, font, ambo, chairs for presider and assembly) as well as the musicians' places and instruments—that none is fixed in place. We also presuppose a flat floor and portable platforms as needed. In addition, we assume that the assembly using such space is relatively small (say not more than 250 people), this being so largely for logistical reasons. We assume a pattern of variation not to exceed three options. This number, as we will argue below, will express the theological/architectural norms well and, practically speaking, will likely not unduly tax the good will of the assembly. Lastly, we assume an assembly which recognizes its own "plasticity," as Louis Bouyer calls it.[10] Such an assembly would see mirrored in its own mobility something of the dynamic character inherent in a people grasped by a "living" God.

While these assumptions undergird what follows, another matter needs clear expression. That is, we assume that "movable" here *does not mean* insubstantial, flimsy or transient-looking furniture—in other words, not "card tables and metal folding chairs." We imagine, instead, substantial, "authentic" furniture able to bear the symbolic weight rightly placed upon it.

We move now to the heart of the matter, the two major influences which converge to become the "stuff" of this exploration. As we hinted earlier in the introductory remarks, the operational norm for our proposed variations is the Christian year, "the sequence of celebrations around specific themes by which the church annually calls to mind the unfolding of God's creative and redemptive activity through Jesus Christ in the Holy Spirit." [11] Of central significance for us are the seasons, "whole chunks of time to which the church gives a particular meaning or mood through the liturgy." [12] Advent, Christmas, Epiphany, Lent, Easter, Pentecost—these are central players in our proposal.

What is attractive about the calendar, in its seasonal expression, is its regularity, predictability, dependability and its duration. Unlike the sanctoral cycle as a pattern for variation or the several sacraments, the duration of the seasons allows the assembly to rehabituate itself, "to live into" the space again, to find "itself" anew in this place of encounter. Briefer periods of time or more sporadic variations would risk merely startling rather than renewing and edifying the assembly. In a season, a "particular meaning" can work its work. And, in a season, some "familiarity" necessary to human habitation can be acquired. [13]

To claim the calendar as the norm by which spatial variation is to be governed is at the same time to claim christology as "the touchstone for what is considered normative in the liturgy," as Mark Searle has put it in another context. [14] And to speak of meanings for the seasons is to speak of the person and the work of Christ communicated in the liturgy and appropriated by the church. The person and work of Christ is at the heart of our liturgy; it is the "root metaphor" for our ritual activity. [15]

Alongside the calendar and its christological frame, we set another interpreter of experience, another formative influence important to our discussion. Suzanne Langer, writing in *Feeling and Form*, speaks of "motifs" as "organizing devices that give the artist's imagination a start"; they "motivate the work . . . drive it forward, and guide its progress." [16] The rhythm of the calendar provides us with one set of motifs, those which emerge from and characterize the seasons. The next issue for our consideration is the motifs for ordering, configuring spaces. Christian Norberg-Schulz provides them.

An Apology for Variable Liturgical Space

Writing in *Meaning in Western Architecture*, Norberg-Schulz observes that "art and religion have common roots and together serve the purpose of making man aware of existential meanings." These meanings are "inherent in daily life, consisting of the relationships between natural and human properties, processes and actions." He goes on to say that such meanings are "necessarily revealed in a particular place and the character of the place is determined by this revelation (i.e., the disclosure of meaning). In other words, the experienced meanings constitute from the very outset an *existential space*, which forms a framework" for human actions.[17] The author then suggests that "it is . . . possible to describe some basic structural properties which are common to all existential spaces. These properties are related to the archetypal relations of primitive symbolism and constitute the point of departure for any further development of spatial images and concepts."[18] These "constituent elements of existential space" Norberg-Schulz names "places, paths and domains."[19] Understood as "relations" more than geographical locations, these will serve us as our second set of "motifs."

Domains constitute the field upon which the other two reside. They "have a unifying function in existential space for they form a relatively unstructured ground on which places and paths appear as more pronounced figures." In one sense, domains are the "remainder," in another, they constitute what is ordinary. *Places* are "centers," the most basic element in existential space, experienced as "insides," and typically round. They are, however, not only "goals or foci" but also "points of departure from which we orient ourselves." *Paths* can be horizontal or vertical; they are relational and interconnective; they give our existential space "a more particular structure."[20]

Now we need to return to the calendar and collate our motifs. In our annual cycle, we have three sorts of seasons: (1) times of preparation, expectation or pilgrimage (Advent and Lent); (2) times of central definition (Christmas season and Epiphany, Easter to Pentecost); and (3) ordinary time (the Epiphany season and the season of Pentecost). Put another way, we have seasons which are pathways, places and domains.

The two schemes—seasonal and relational/spatial—converge and give mutual expression and reinforcement.

Thus, we come to the suggestion that the varying of liturgical spaces be done according to this reading of the calendar and that it be expressed around the several spatial motifs.

In the final section of this essay we will attempt explicit proposals for accomplishing this. Before moving to that most perilous work, we should return to a point made earlier which can be made more clearly now.

Earlier, in our introductory remarks, we noted that the keeping of the calendar "allows the tensions or dialectics in our faith, and in our liturgical life, to be expressed with integrity and not have to be disposed of in some too-easy accommodation." It could just as well be argued that the use of variable space avails the same kind of possibilities. We have suggested that to the extent that the configuration of the liturgical space projects/contains/expresses particular meaning, variable liturgical space would do so more richly than would a permanent fixed space. This being so, the variable ordering of the space, when viewed from the broad perspective of the whole annual cycle, could convey more fully (rather than resolve artificially or falsely) the dialectics or paradoxes on which we frankly depend. Recall, for a moment, the unhappy choices one is forced to make between *domus Dei/domus ecclesiae;* interiority/exteriority, pilgrimage (as longing, expectation, preparation)/arrival (as fulfillment, satisfaction); plasticity/stability; immanence/transcendence. Or, put another way, as the Irish Bishops' Conference said some years ago, "the rhythm of the Christian life, development and renunciation, involvement and detachment, cross and resurrection, needs to be expressed in a visual sense."[21] Variable liturgical space would greatly enable the accomplishment of this clear vision.

Some Spatial Examples

"The important point . . . in a new church is not to arrange as well as possible a set of impersonal objects (the altar/table, the pulpit, the baptismal font, etc.), but to give form and shape to a living, praying, offering community . . . "[22] Making suggestions about "form and shape" is what remains, the variable ordering of the liturgical space. The question is, what arrangement(s) will best serve as suitable/appropriate settings for our three "motifs," paths, places, domain? In speaking of each of these, we will always be concerned not only with the relationship of altar/table, ambo, font and presider, but also with the setting of the assembly. In fact, insofar as the character or "texture" of the several settings is concerned, it may be this last which is most important. So, into the minefield!

Domains: By our earlier reckoning, the season of Pentecost is a domain in our calendar. Since this is ordinary time, the ordering of the space during this period should be whatever constitutes the normal or typical arrangement for the assembly. This being so (and given the norms and assumptions outlined earlier), various arrangements might serve. The decisions made for this time might better be made *after* determination had been made for the other seasons, since their specialness is the necessary contrast to the ordinariness of this longest season.

For the purposes of our considerations, we might use the plan whereby the altar/table and ambo (put in proper balance) are placed with the assembly on three sides, either in sets of straight rows or in a fan-shape. In either case, the font could be placed near the entry and in association with an aisle. If straight rows were used, this arrangement would create open spaces in the "corners." One of these spaces would properly hold the font.

Given the fact that for our work at the moment, we are imagining no dictatorial axis to the room itself, the setting could be worked such that its relationship to the point of entry could also vary. Care should always be taken to locate the font so that its powerful theological and symbolic importance is attested, with reference both to the point of entry and to the assembly.

Paths: Although each has its own special character, the seasons of Advent and Lent are both seasons of preparation, anticipation, pilgrimage. Each has about it the sense of movement toward fulfillment. How best to convey this?

The first possibility might be to create the kind of setting for the assembly which Frederic Debuyst has called a "static procession."[23] This would be two narrow ranks of chairs, set in strict rows, divided by an axial middle aisle. The assembly would face "east," the altar/table and ambo (being in proper balance) located at the east end. The placement of the altar/table and ambo might be at some remove from the assembly. The presider might (even) pray the Great Thanksgiving facing east.

A second alternative would be the setting of the assembly in choir, several straight rows of chairs facing each other across a central axial aisle. Whereas the first proposal sets the people facing the "goal" (so to say) of their pilgrimage, this second one fixes them upon the pathway itself. In choir, the matter of the placement of the altar/table and ambo is opened a bit wider than in the first alternative. Here the central aisle might hold the ambo at one end (say the "west") and the altar/table at the other ("east"). In this arrangement, the "pilgrimage" itself would be marked by the visual and physical movement from the ambo (the focus of the liturgy of the word) to the altar/table (the focus of the liturgy of the table). As the assembly stood for the Great Thanksgiving, they would stand, more or less, in lines, as if "pilgrims."

With either of these pathway possibilities, since neither Advent nor Lent is a conventional baptismal season, the font could remain in its "customary" place.

Places: The definitional seasons are Christmas-Epiphany and the Great Fifty Days. Since, as Norberg-Schulz observed, "places" are typically round, we can begin our discussion by considering the circle. Although there are powerful examples of circular liturgical spaces, Metropolitan Cathedral, Liverpool, being one such, significant objections have been raised against the circle, objections we must consider briefly as a way of moving on.[24]

The criticisms of the circle are typically three. First, the assembly ordered in a circle is viewed as too inward-looking, too neglecting of "the world." Secondly, the circle-as-metaphor, complete and "perfect" as it is, is viewed as likely to misguide the assembly as regards its own incompleteness. Thirdly, for practical reasons, ordering the assembly in full circle would require some folks to be behind the presider and preacher, a bad thing in the eye of the critic.

An Apology for Variable Liturgical Space

From the point of view of this essay, only the third criticism is compelling. The power of the first two objections is mitigated in large measure by the seasonal varying of the space. That is, the critics of the circle, under objection one and two, assume a permanent arrangement, one that would constantly "teach" or "mean" the same thing. Varying the space would not only soften these objections but also take the remaining negative residue of the objection and make a virtue of it, through contrast.

So, in commending the circle for our definitional seasons, only the third objection need inform our design. This argues against placing the altar/table and ambo in the center. It also argues against closing the circle behind the altar/table and ambo. At the same time, the space needs to convey a sense of vertical axis rather than horizontal, this latter being more appropriate to the seasons of pilgrimage than the seasons of fulfillment.

Perhaps, then, our best option is to choose a "rotund" U-shape, broken at appropriate aisles and deep enough for the center to be obvious. At the top of the "U," the east end, the altar/table and ambo could sit in proper balance, placed so that no one in the assembly was behind presider or preacher, even though these foci were "inside" rather than on the perimeter of the arc. For the Great Fifty Days, beginning with the Easter Vigil, the font would be placed within the circle, say at the "west" end, the paschal candle its companion. And although the axial sense of the space should be vertical, the font's placement might still be at an aisle, with reference to whichever is the primary entry to the room. During Christmas through the feast of Epiphany, the font would remain in its customary location, being set within the circle when appropriate, e.g., the Baptism of Jesus.

This is all we can say at present. Many possibilities remain to be imagined and explored. What we have suggested is obviously abstract in its way and disregarding of many issues, both technical and liturgical. At the same time, the point of the exercise is the fashioning of a rationale which might support variety rather than the fixing of the several patterns. The actual settling of patterns is clearly the appropriate business of local planners and designers, artists and musicians, theologians and liturgists.

What we propose here obviously needs to fit into a building. The proposal assumes a built environment which accepts flexibility and variation as a norm or as something given. Our concentration on the furniture does not mean to disregard or neglect the power and influence of the room itself. Puzzling about the room is simply beyond our current intention.

The last word goes to Marchita Mauck. Although she writes from a context somewhat different than ours, what she says is a seemly conclusion to this essay.

> "The goal [of liturgical space-making] is to create spaces that honor the holiness of God's people and shape their experience of being church. Spaces that lift our hearts, that enable the perception of the presence of God in each other and the things of this world, are spaces that confirm our identity as well as convert us, that guide us to new points of view. We must create spaces whose rhythms will draw us into the cadences of life and death, until we come at last to the wholeness and unity of God' s presence."[25]

---

1. Rudolf Schwarz, *The Church Incarnate*, translated by C. Harris (Chicago: Henry Regnery, 1958), p. 198.

2. See, for example, James F. White, *An Introduction to Christian Worship* (Nashville: Abingdon, 1980), p. 95.

3. See, for example, Richard Vosko, *Through the Eye of the Rose Window* (Sarasota, FL: Resources Publications, 1981), p. 45; *Environment and Art in Catholic Worship* (Washington, DC: U.S. Catholic Conference, 1978), p. 65; J.G. Davies, *The Secular Use of Church Buildings* (New York: Seabury, 1968).

4. Two articles present the rationale for the multipurpose church: J.G. Davies, "The Role of the Church in the Twentieth Century" and Gilbert Cope, "Church Building in the Twentieth Century," both published in *Research Bulletin 1967* (Birmingham, UK: Institute for the Study of Worship and Religious Architecture, 1967).

5. William H. Willimon, *The Service of God* (Nashville: Abingdon, 1983), pp. 48–72; Christopher Kiesling, "The Formative Influence of Liturgy," *Studies in Formative Spirituality* 3 (1982), pp. 377–385. I have treated this idea in

"Scripture, Liturgy and the Jews: A Problematic in Jewish-Christian Relations," forthcoming in *The Journal of Ecumenical Studies*. (It is contained in the present volume.)

6. "Response: The Berakah Award for 1981," *Worship* 55 (1981), p. 363.

7. "Kyrie Eleison and the Entrance Rite of the Roman Eucharist," *Worship* 60 (1986), p. 347.

8. "Holy Places and Christian Theology," *Liturgy: Holy Places* 3:4 (Fall, 1983), p. 12.

9. See Kenneth Murta, "An Interim Report on Research into the Use of Church Buildings Where the Design has been Influenced by the Liturgical Movement," *Research Bulletin 1970* (Birmingham, UK: Institute for the Study of Worship and Religious Architecture, 1970), p. 40.

10. *Liturgy and Architecture* (Notre Dame: The University of Notre Dame Press, 1967), p. 96.

11. Kiesling, previously cited, p. 377.

12. *Ibid.*, p. 378.

13. In this regard, attention should be called to Joseph Fete, "The Building and Remodeling of Churches and High Anxiety," *Liturgical Apostolate* ([RC] Diocese of Columbus, Winter, 1986).

14. "The Pedagogical Function of the Liturgy," *Worship* 55 (1981), p. 358.

15. See Patrick Collins, *More Than Meets the Eye* (New York: Paulist, 1983), p. 51f.

16. (London: Routledge and Kegan Paul, 1953), p. 69.

17. (New York: Rizzoli, 1980), p. 223.

18. *Ibid.*

19. *Ibid.*, p. 224.

20. *Ibid.*

21. Cited in James Notebaart, "In Pursuit of Truth and Beauty," *Liturgy: Holy Places* 3:4 (Fall, 1983), p. 57.

22. Frederic Debuyst, *Modern Architecture and Christian Celebration* (Richmond, VA: John Knox Press, 1968), p. 58.

23. Previously cited, p. 45.

24. See, for example, Bouyer, previously cited, p. 93; Marianne Micks, *The Future Present* (New York: Seabury, 1970), p. 131f; W. Jardine Grisbrooke,

"The Shape of the Liturgical Assembly: Some Third Thoughts," *Research Bulletin 1972* (Birmingham, UK: Institute for the Study of Worship and Religious Architecture, 1972), p. 41.

25. "Buildings that House the Church," *Liturgy: Dressing the Church* 5:4 (Spring, 1986), p. 33.

Chapter Nine

Theology and Liturgical Space
Saying What We Mean[1]

As theology always arises from, and subsequently helps to form, a specific local context, I have decided to envision here a clearly defined community, a building committee: a group of people, resident and active in an Episcopal parish, who are "in the mood" to design, reorder or build a liturgical space. With appropriate variations, my reflections can then be applied to many other contexts.

To picture the situation so concretely is intended to help me focus, not on what to say, but on how to say it. It is important to speak about theological matters, but eventually practical decisions must be made and often by pragmatic people.

Once "in the mood," a building committee often does not know exactly what to do next. Helping building committees in Episcopal parishes is really the purview of the local diocesan commission on architecture, through which the parochial committee presumably can be informed and equipped to proceed. Consequently, I will pass over such matters as the architectural process, choosing an architect, finances, written resources and committee dynamics in favor of something more basic and yet more elusive, namely, theology.

The Episcopal Experience[2]

In the Episcopal Church, liturgical life and practice are rooted in Scripture and tradition as mediated to us through the Book of Common Prayer [BCP]. The current revision of the BCP is a truly wonderful document, surely the richest and most varied in the series of revisions that has continued through 400 years. Whatever claims we may want to make for our liturgical theology, our liturgical practice and our liturgical spaces must finally be tested by the Prayer Book.

In regard to liturgical planning, therefore, the situation in the Episcopal Church is quite different from that in the Roman Catholic Church. The Roman Church is guided by the Constitution on the Sacred Liturgy, now twenty-five years old, and the official and semi-official directives it spawned, including [in the United States] the works of the National Conference of Catholic Bishops on music and environment and art.[3] We Episcopalians, on the other hand, are left more or less to our own devices, that is, to diocesan, parochial or private management of the Prayer Book's assumptions.

This is why Marion Hatchett's paper, "The Architectural Implications of the Book of Common Prayer," is so helpful and unique.[4] While the Roman Church produced a handsome book, attractively illustrated with the work of Frank Kacmarcik and documented with references to the constitution on the liturgy and other sources of semi-holy writ, we have relied on a six-page typescript circulated almost secretly.[5] Hence, the relevance and necessity of considerations such as these [contained in this address].

Liturgical Space and Christian Identity

As a way of beginning to explore some theological dimensions that should be considered by a building committee, let me say what I understand a liturgical space to be. First, and this is perhaps obvious, a liturgical space is a shelter—a shelter for the worship of the church, its praises, songs and offerings. As such, it accomplishes the same practical and necessary things all shelters do: it protects, encloses, perhaps enfolds. It is an "inside" that is distinct from an "outside," and this is so even if the "inside" is found outdoors.

Second, a liturgical space is a place where the church, encountering God, sets forth its own self-understanding most clearly. Since our liturgical space is our ritual space, and since our ritual life more than anything else gives us identity, our liturgical space is our ground for identity. On ritual ground we tell our story, enact our identity, recreate and nourish our memory. Liturgical spaces are holy places because they are places of encounter and ritual.

Third, and this point derives immediately from the above, a liturgical space is a place for bodies and what bodies do in public. Such spaces are places for movement and sensation. They are not places of *dis*-embodiment, but the opposite.

Fourth, and last, a liturgical space is a setting where the church in some measure tastes and sees something of the reign of God. It is a place where the norms and expectations of God's reign are acted out, where we see and know not so much how things are but how they ought to be, where the language of love and justice translate each other without remainder.

Function, Style and Meaning

It was the American architect Louis Henry Sullivan whose view of architecture was captured in the aphorism, "form follows function." His statement stimulates our reflection in two ways. One way to look at "function" is to ask, "What do we need the space for? What do we do in it?" This is easily answered. In our liturgical space, we gather, stand, kneel, sit, see, are seen, read, sing, speak, listen, play music, are silent, touch, move, eat, wash, promise, bless, commend, heal, anoint and lay hands on people, and this list could be extended. These answers to the function question are activities for which we must make place. The spatial order must be directed and shaped by what we do.

There is, however, another way to view "function" that leads us more deeply into our topic. If the question of function requires us to ask what we do, it also leads us to ask, "What does (or should) this space mean?"

This is the second piece of functional work a liturgical space has to do. It has to "mean" something. Now clearly, "meaning" is an elusive notion, for meanings are rich, multiple, open. It is not my intention to inhibit that richness or reduce its multiplicity. Indeed, I want to leave the explication and elaboration of meaning in local hands—planners, designers, artists, musicians, theologians and liturgists, people resident in congregations. It is their particular business. It is my intention, though, to provoke reflection about meaning in relation to several theological issues. I should say also that I am not secretly moving us toward a particular vocabulary of architectural style (e.g., Gothic, romanesque, postmodern), but toward a theological vocabulary related to specific categories. Consequently, I would urge the building committee about to fashion a program for or with an architect, to reflect on a series of theological ideas to help shape their decisions.

The importance of these considerations is best understood when we remember that in the liturgy, Sunday by Sunday, the body of Christ is recreated. The setting, the environment in which the liturgy is celebrated, is where the body of Christ is formed, edified, nourished. Liturgical spaces are profound teachers of the nature of the church, and they are central to the process of formation. Thus, theological deliberation about the liturgical space, about spatial expression, about "meaning," is fundamental to the making of Christians.

The theological categories I would press on a building committee are four: God, the church, the sacraments and creation. We will consider each in turn. Although I will invariably express an opinion, my real hope is to persuade committees to ponder these matters for themselves as a prelude to design.

Liturgical Space and Ideas of God

There is a particular sense of God that one gets in a liturgical space. It may have to do with the size and shape of the place, the location of the altar table, the height of the ceiling. Whatever it is, we know and feel something about God in that place. Sensitivity to this feeling is an issue for design.

Theology and Liturgical Space

The God who is high and lifted up, the one who is Pantokrator, ruler of all, creator of all, judge of all, who adorns the domes of orthodox churches and the ceiling of the Sistine Chapel—this God is also the one who dwelt among us, who took the form of a slave, the one who is with us. This God is the one whom we praise, the God of our experience and our faith. The question is how do we express this faith in our liturgical spaces? In our designs, both the transcendence and the immanence of God need thoughtful reflections and expression. We must take into account two sets of balances. The first is the balance between grandeur and humility or servanthood; the second, the balance between the idea that the liturgical space is God's house and the notion that it is our house. These two balances are intimately related, and both have similar implications.

The balance (sometimes tension) between grandeur and servanthood is an item of business that has been on the church's agenda since the time of Constantine. We seem to be almost predisposed to build liturgical spaces "for the glory of God." This disposition has expressed itself over and over again, typically in monumental buildings, towering spaces richly adorned, great holy caverns. The finest in human craft and art is prominently displayed in these places, and visitors feel the awesomeness of their space and splendor. These are the buildings of Christendom.

The rightful urge to praise God in wood, stone and glass is, at the same time, disciplined by the church's perpetual call to service and stewardship, the care we are responsible to give God in the world. Economic justice and God's prejudice in favor of the poor and outcast may require more reverential simplicity and less grandeur—always keeping in mind, of course, that this is a question of balance, not of alternatives or opposites. Our efforts to maintain this balance can be supported by the reminder that the church's purpose is assisted by its buildings, but to build buildings is *not* the purpose of the church.

Attached directly to this first balance is the second: the balance between our sense that the liturgical space is the house of God and the idea that it is the house of God's people. If we imagine the church to be the house of God, the mountain of the Lord, the very gate of heaven, we will likely move in our thinking toward either a regal metaphor (i.e., the basilica) or a temple metaphor, perhaps a throne room or a shrine. Under the influence of these metaphors, the character of the space would be awe-inspiring, holy, perhaps mysterious, making much of God and God's transcendence, power, majesty.

If instead we imagine the liturgical space to be the house of God's people, a space with a more social, human character, then we will likely move toward a domestic metaphor. Here the interactive character of the community will assume a higher priority than it does when our thinking is influenced by other metaphors.

My own thinking leans more heavily toward the domestic end than toward the awesome end, but choosing between them is not the point. The point is the necessary consideration of both. Somewhere, perched and balanced among such reflections, will arise a view of God that will inform our design.

It might be possible and appropriate for certain churches within a local area or a diocese to serve as places of awe, places to which pilgrimages are made, while the more typical parochial churches are more domestic in texture and character. The first model might be a role for the cathedral, though we must be careful not to make an overly exclusive association between the "house of God" and the house of the bishop.

Ecclesiology in Wood and Stone

As designers need to ponder the spatial implications of their view of God, so also with regard to the nature of the church. The church gathered for the liturgy is perhaps its primary manifestation, and how we gather invariably shows forth something of what we imagine the nature of the church to be.

One liturgical legacy that we have inherited, and now need to shed, is our clericalized liturgy. The notion that the liturgy is the priest's work is the principal informant for many liturgical spaces. This hierarchical view has been expressed again and again, in a variety of times and architectural styles. In our time, happily, the liturgical revitalization of the churches has reminded us that the primary ministry of the church is that of the baptized. The liturgy is rooted in the community of the baptized, a community in which the liturgical roles and responsibilities are distributed for the sake of order and the necessary functioning of the group. This order, in turn, is distinguishable from the idea of hierarchy. Robert W. Hovda has put it this way:

> The honesty appropriate to a gathering of sinners like ourselves suggests that any pretense, affectation or deceit are just too silly for words. The varieties of ministries which such an assembly needs for liturgical celebration is a matter of respect for different competencies, different gifts and talents, different forms of training, different calls and commissionings from the assembly as a whole. Those different ministries are *not* a matter of higher or lower, superior and inferior. Baptism into the priesthood of Christ and a common sinful humanity is the basis of our egalitarianism.[6]

Sensitivity to matters of ecclesiology suggests at least three considerations. First, a one-room plan is likely to convey or represent this understanding of the church better than any other. The typical neogothic configuration, on the other hand, involves three rooms (one for the faithful, one for the choir and one for the clergy) and hierarchical elevations. This will no longer serve. This conclusion carries with it the necessary abandonment of the old language of "nave, chancel and sanctuary," even though we have yet to find good replacements for these terms.

Second, the order of space needs to testify to the corporate, rather than individual, use of the room. The ecclesiology that informs the Book of Common Prayer is an ecclesiology of corporate prayer. The liturgical space is intended for corporate, public use, not for private, individual use. For the latter, an oratory is appropriate, a place for quiet, private prayer, a space set apart from the primary liturgical space that encourages interrelatedness and visual contact rather than isolation and distinction.

Third, a communal ecclesiology requires that we ponder carefully the matter of access. In the most obvious sense, the inclusive nature of our

145

understanding of the church requires of us a space that can be used by people of all sorts and conditions. The physically handicapped need as ready access to the space as those whose handicaps are less obvious, which is yet another argument against hierarchical elevations. Visual and auditory access are also crucial. Our liturgical space needs no secret places, no places that cannot be seen by all, no places from which speakers or singers cannot be heard. Going to church and being relegated to the back of a transept is a kind of excommunication no one needs.

Such concerns about ecclesiology suggest to me that the typical configuration, which seems to be modeled on a bus or perhaps a theater, is less likely to serve than something more circular. Ordering the room so that people can see each other as well as they can see the traditional liturgical centers may help teach the church about its humanity and its neighborliness, and it will certainly help to prevent the sense of isolation that many churches evoke.

Sacraments and Ritual Centers

The sacraments lie at the heart of Christian liturgical practice. The BCP is quite direct in declaring that Holy Eucharist is the liturgy proper to Sundays and festivals and that Holy Baptism is full initiation into the body of Christ, suitably celebrated within the gathered community. Each of these sacraments has its physical aspect and its particular ritual object, the altar table and the font.

Preaching (proclamation) has never been counted among the traditional sacraments of the church (though its institution and warrant in Scripture are quite as strong as baptism). Nevertheless, its centrality to the rites could hardly be greater. The reading and proclamation of Scripture are a virtually unexceptionable part of our eucharistic and baptismal liturgies. Hence, the ritual object associated with proclamation, the ambo, also needs our serious attention. Surely it is true to say that God's graciousness toward us is mediated at font, altar table and ambo.

The challenge to the building committee is the visual or symbolic integration of these three ritual centers. I call this a challenge because the force of convention is against this balance or integration. Peter Hammond, an English [Anglican] priest and writer on ecclesiastical architecture, said some years ago, "The building must be designed from the altar outwards . . . The altar, and its relationship to the worshiping community, must be the strong point for the layout of the eucharistic room."[7] The current revision of the BCP argues, I believe, for a rather different conclusion.

A glance at the make-up of the liturgy of Holy Eucharist clearly reveals that the rite is composed of two parts, the Word of God and Holy Communion. If we accept Hammond's idea that the room should be built to accommodate the rite, then ritual objects that focus these two parts of the rite would provide the "proper starting point[s] for the layout of the eucharistic room." That would mean, it seems to me, that the altar table would not be viewed in isolation from the ambo or vice versa. Neither, taken singly, would be the central focus of the room.

Similarly, since the BCP clearly associates Holy Baptism with the eucharistic liturgy and with the special festival days, the relationship of font, altar table and ambo invites reconsideration. Placing the font at the entry to the room is sensible as far as the symbolism of initiation or admission to the community is concerned, but its typical location behind the congregation needs further thought. One solution is to make the entry area large enough to accommodate the assembly, so that all can gather there for the baptismal liturgy and then move to the altar table for the liturgy of Holy Communion.

It is also appropriate to recall that our sacramental theology imposes on us the responsibility of authenticity. Since the sacraments have entirely to do with God's disposition to use material things to our good, the least we can do is to make them available in sufficient physical and symbolic proportions. This means that we should not have to puzzle over the existence and character of the bread and wine or water. Droplets of water secreted away in an opaque bowl hardly convey baptismal power. The visual or physical integrity of these material things, as material, is basic to the impact of the sacraments. Liturgical spaces and liturgical objects need to be fashioned with this in mind.

147

The Rhythm of Creation

I have called this last theological category "creation" because I want to consider how liturgical space and its use is related to time and the rhythm of nature. As a sacramental people, we are persuaded, as God is, that creation is good. We have come to depend on its urges and patterns, though we may also struggle mightily to contain or redirect them. What I want to dwell on for the moment is the rhythm of creation, the rhythm of life really, the rhythm we know as activity moving toward rest, fluidity moving toward stability and back again. This is the oscillation necessary for our human continuance. We recognize ourselves in it.

This rhythm is present in our liturgical life in several ways. Take the calendar, for example, in whose patterns of festivals we see the church moving from "ordinary" to "extraordinary" and back again; or take the role of silence in the eucharist, where rest and reflection are invited to vary the experience of mind and body. These patterns or rhythms in creation and the liturgy are health-giving and natural.

Pondering these vital and necessary rhythms moves us to think about change itself. Change is often treated as a fearful menace unless it plays into our hands. And that is my point: change and variety do, I think, play into our hands. The rhythm of the Christian year, like the rhythm of the earth, helps us be who we are, moment to moment. Calendar keeping grants us memory and identity. Variation is formative, creative; invariability often works to mislead or misrepresent.

All this is said to lure designers into considering a liturgical space that is variable and flexible; a space informed by strong theological, liturgical and aesthetic norms; a space varied moderately and under the influence of the calendar and good sense. Such a space would allow the genuine flexibility of the BCP to be set in motion. To ignore its intended flexibility would be serious business, disadvantageous to the liturgical community and the cause of an impoverished formative influence for the church. Spatial flexibility also has the advantage of leaving the future relatively unburdened by the past we build for it now.

In a strange way, discussions about liturgical change, spatial and textual, call to mind our struggle over the nature of God. Here we return to matters begun earlier. When treating things liturgical, we seem to want our texts and settings to bear an analogous resemblance to the God we imagine. Our image of God, however, is all too often informed by a Greek philosophical idea, which is also enshrined in some places in the New Testament: God is the same, unchanging, immutable, impassible. What would our theology be like if our analogous image were otherwise? What if our analogue were the God of Genesis, who creates, walks in gardens, sets rainbows? Or the God of the psalmist, an active, vigilant, social God who is far more than an abstract principle? This is surely the God who keeps promises and is trustworthy and faithful, but who is not "the same" in the sense of being immutable. I suspect this is the God whom Jesus would recognize as "Father."[8]

In addition to my hope that designers will find the variability of nature and the vitality of God sufficient stimuli to consider flexibility, our reflections on "creation" suggest some other directions.

Taking creation seriously means avoiding sham in design and materials, and designing with nature as an ally. Surely these two points are self-evident, but I will intensify them with negative examples. As regards sham, let me cite Coventry Cathedral in England. Heralded by many as a harbinger of the future when it was completed in 1962, it is in fact an art museum built on Gothic lines and used for liturgical purposes. Looking at its interior, one sees along the aisles what appear to be columns and arches, made of steel, reaching from floor to ceiling. Closer inspection tells otherwise. These "columns and arches" are not only not structural, they are not really columns and arches at all. They are decorations. They do not support the ceiling, but are suspended from the ceiling. They do not actually reach the ground, and each is held in place at the bottom by a small steel pin that rises out of the floor to meet it lest it move. This is, bluntly, architectural sham.

The notion of taking nature as an ally invites designers and planners to be very thoughtful about excluding the outdoors from view by means of colored glass, especially representational glass. My example here is a small chapel from whose window might have been seen mountains and the Pacific Ocean. Instead, opaque colored glass had been placed in the opening, depicting Christ, lamp in hand, knocking at a door. Along the bottom of the window, again in opaque colored glass, the mountains and ocean obscured by the window are clearly represented. Here nature was not enlisted as an ally, but apparently needed "improvement."

Clearly the interplay of indoors and outdoors needs care. I know of dreadful examples where care was not taken, where the outdoors overwhelms and disables the liturgy. Certainly one must focus attention and manage light and shadow. It is God whom we praise and adore, not nature; and, unquestionably, the luminescence of beautiful glass can be a powerful stimulant to liturgical piety. But all the same, we must not give the impression that we regard stained glass as more "religious" than the earth.

God, the church, the sacraments, creation. There is much more to be said. Perhaps it is best for me simply to say again that liturgical spaces are powerful teachers. They teach the church about the church, about who we are, how we work, what we do, what is important to us, who is important to us; and they teach us about God. This is why we must know the BCP and under its good influences do our theological homework very well.

W.H. Auden rather playfully suggested that the work of the architect is "to puzzle the unborn."[9] Not so for liturgical architecture! You and I must see to it that we say what we mean. Then, God willing, presumably we will mean what we say.

---

1. The contents of this article were originally given in an address to the Episcopal Diocese of Los Angeles Conference on Environment and Art for Worship in May, 1987. Other speakers were Frank Kacmarcik and S. Anita Stauffer. The address was modestly edited by the staff at *Liturgy* so as to broaden the application. What is printed here is the *Liturgy* rendition.

2. The editors of *Liturgy* introduced these headings. I have chosen to keep them but have altered several to achieve more congruence with the text.

3. Bishops' Committee on the Liturgy, *Music in Catholic Worship* (Washington, D.C.: United States Catholic Conference, 1972) and *Environment and Art in Catholic Worship* (Washington, D.C.: United States Catholic Conference, 1978).

4. Marion Hatchett, "The Architectural Implications of the Book of Common Prayer," Standing Liturgical Commission [of the Episcopal Church] Occasional Paper Number 7, December 1984.

5. Hatchett's article, along with others, was subsequently published in book form, under the title *The Occasional Papers of the Standing Liturgical Commission,* Collection Number One (New York: Standing Liturgical Commission, 1984).

6. Bishop's Committee on the Liturgy, "It Begins with the Assembly," in *The Environment for Worship* (Washington, D.C.: United States Catholic Conference, 1980), p. 41.

7. Peter Hammond, *Liturgy and Architecture* (New York: Columbia University, 1961), p. 35.

8. See William Seth Adams, "An Apology for Variable Liturgical Space," *Worship* 61/3 (May 1987). (It is contained in the present volume.)

9. W.H. Auden, "Thanksgiving for a Habitat, I. Program: The Birth of Architecture, in *W.H. Auden Selected Poems,* ed. Edward Mendelson (New York: Random House Vintage, 1979), p. 252.

Chapter Ten

The Place of the Dead

*Christian Burial and the
Liturgical Environment*

The relationship between the liturgical rites of the church and the liturgical environment is both a rich and subtle one. The more care we take in our liturgical theology and our exploration of the sacraments,

the more the findings of that exploration need to express themselves in the place where those same rites and sacraments are celebrated. This attention is required because the liturgical space plays such a powerful and enduring role in the formation of the liturgical community which uses it.

It is increasingly common for the liturgical, theological and pragmatic necessities of eucharist, proclamation and baptism to exert their happy influences on building committees and designers of liturgical spaces. The spaces thus created are supple testimony not only to the insight of designers, but also to the centrality of table, ambo, and font, and to the needs of the assembly and the one who presides.

For the purposes of the current remarks, we intend to stretch the normal limits of design considerations and look at the relationship of the liturgical environment and the burial of the dead. In doing so, we will look briefly at three aspects of the matter—first, the relationship of the liturgical space to the rite itself; secondly, the actual place of burial; and, thirdly, the relationship between the remembrance of the dead and the continuing formation of the liturgical community.

It seems curious to say so, but, as the Book of Common Prayer suggests, " . . . Christians are properly buried from the church." (p. 468) It is curious because one would think it so obvious—obviously the community of the faithful gathers to remember and celebrate the life of one who has died, and, equally obviously, that remembrance and celebration happen logically where the church's other celebrations occur. Yet, in some traditions and for many people, the experience of this final rite of passage is increasingly associated with chapels in funeral homes and not with the church building. So, perhaps, the first thing for us to say is to urge as forcefully as possible that the rite of the burial of the dead be returned to the church building, to the liturgical space. This is the place where the ecclesial memory of the community is set in motion, where the primordial stories are told and re-told, where the central signs and symbols of the faith are in evidence.

With reference to the space itself, though the specific requirements here are modest, the space must clearly accommodate the particular needs of the rite and the community, as these needs express themselves for the burial office. From the tradition of which I am a part, this would mean an entry and/or gathering space that would allow for the reception of the body (casket), the act that typically begins the liturgy of burial. This reception is accompanied by prayer and the action of draping the casket with a pall. Under the best of circumstances, those who received the body would include not only the presider and those who would assist with the draping, but pall bearers and family members, as well as members of the congregation. All of these persons would then participate in the entry procession.

Following the reception, the procession from the entry to some central location (often a place near the altar/table) requires a sufficiently broad aisle that this solemn movement can be accomplished with ease and visual clarity. Typically accompanied by the recitation or singing of words of great power ("I am Resurrection and I am Life, says the Lord . . ."), this procession is a sign of the "passage" and "pilgrimage" which lie at the heart of the rite. The procession, therefore, needs to be seen.

The placement of the casket needs to be such that those present can see it and such that it does not become an obstacle to movement in the rite. If, for example, the eucharist is celebrated and if the liturgical room is such that the casket sits at the foot of the chancel stairs, as it might in a Gothic-like building, then the casket can become an impediment to those who move toward the altar/table for communion.

At the same time, consideration needs to be given to the inclusion of the casket within the liturgical community as well as within the liturgical action. Our faith persuades us that those who die in the Lord remain in communion not only with God but also with the living, so the physical exclusion of their mortal remains contradicts our theological intent. That is to say, solving the "obstacle" problem must not result in the exclusion of the casket.

Since "[t]he liturgy of the dead is an Easter liturgy, [BCP, 507]," wherever the casket is placed, it should be accompanied by the pascal candle, lighted. The candle could be carried in the entry procession and placed in its stand, next to the casket, as the casket itself arrives at its proper place. If carried in, the candle might also be carried from the room as the casket is removed to the burial place.

All of these environmental details need to be considered at the design level. For our purposes, these kinds of details lead us, in turn, to consider the actual burial place and the connection between the remembrance of the dead and the formation of the liturgical community.

The history of Christian burial practices lays out before us the church's increasing interest in the place of burial. In the earliest life of the church, burial places were outside the city walls, as was the civil custom of the times. However, as time passed and our theology matured, we began to do two things that changed our sense of the rightful placement of the dead. Firstly, we began to meet at burial grounds for commemorative prayer, the celebrating of saintly lives at the burial site. Secondly, we began to build churches in association with burial grounds, in order to house and shelter our prayers and commemorations. Over time, these churches and burial places were included *inside* the geographical limits of the city or town, as these communities grew around them. The town thus came to surround the burial place and the liturgical place associated with burial became an integral part of urban life. It came to be, then, that the living were accompanied in their daily urban life by reminders of the dead. Burial places were no longer relegated to locations outside the walls—hidden, remote, removed. In a world in which the lines between visible and invisible, between the spirits of the living and the dead, were blurred, the sense of the companionship of our holy dead must have been very powerful, the sense of the presence of the communion of saints almost palpable.

In our time, many of us suffer the deprivation of such powerful and palpable reminders. To be sure, there are plenty of cemeteries which dot the landscape, but very few of them exist in any physical or geographical association with the liturgical community. For most of us, the churchyard is not a burial ground, even though, well into the 18th century, this association would have been our common inheritance.

In recent years, an increasing interest has arisen in returning, in some way, to this earlier practice. This interest usually expresses itself in the design and construction of columbaria, burial places within the confines of the church building or its environs, intended to receive the cremated remains of the dead. One such example is the floor of the chapel of Christ Church Cathedral in St. Louis, the Episcopal cathedral. The pavers which comprise the floor cover the tops of the burial niches and bear the names and life-dates of the persons whose cremated remains are kept below them. The Episcopal Church of the Holy Spirit, Lake Forest, Illinois, a creatively reordered neo-Gothic building built at the turn of the century, has recently added a sizable memorial chapel which adjoins the principal liturgical space and houses a large number of niches with space available for names and dates. In both of these examples, the room which houses the columbarium is a room intended to be used, visited, enjoyed by the living.

In other instances, outdoor gardens serve as the locus for the burial of the faithful, either by means of columbaria or by direct interment into

155

the ground itself. (Direct interment is my own wish upon my death.) Such places serve not only as burial places but also places for contemplation or social interaction. If such a garden possessed a pool or fountain, it could well be used for baptism. A similar possibility exists in an interior space. A columbarium could be built in an extant baptistry, or a baptismal space could be incorporated into an area designated for a columbarium. In any such instance, where better to enact and accomplish baptismal death and resurrection than in a burial ground, surrounded by the living and the dead?

More important, however, than any of these benefits ancillary to the actual burial of the dead, is the role that such places themselves would play in the formation of the liturgical community. At the very heart of our liturgical life and our liturgical formation is the work of remembrance. The liturgy is our "remembrancer," our storyteller, our memory-bearer. The liturgy gathers up the past and re-presents it to us now—its effects, its influences, its impact, its benefits. And in this remembrance, we hear the narration of our identity. What the liturgy remembers with power shapes us, forms us, identifies and describes us. The remembrance of the liturgy protects us from a kind of amnesia, and the calendar of commemorations is clearly a central agent of these acts of recollection.

Throughout the year, it is the custom of the church to remember before God, our holy dead—people whose lives give definition to our hopes, people whose lives give shape to our intentions, people whose lives give substance to our identity. We, the church, hold these in sacred memory. It would be a wonderful aid to this work of remembrance if our liturgical work were done in a setting which was common to the living and the dead. This, it seems to me, is the strongest argument for the return of burial places to the church grounds and buildings. The presence of these reminders of the lives of "the saints" would, as it were, have their way with us. With subtle and enduring power, they would remind us of God's promise about death, a promise made to the living by one who has risen.

Further, if the liturgical community were to celebrate God's saving activity in physical proximity to the burial place, and if we were to proclaim in such a place our convictions that death has been overcome, how better could we declare to a *death-denying* world our intent to be faithfully *death-defying?* Surely, it would prove a remarkable testimony!

The burial office in the Book of Common Prayer contains the following language, part of an anthem borrowed from the Orthodox tradition: "All of us go down to the dust; yet even at the grave we make our song: Alleluia, alleluia, alleluia." (p. 499) If burial places were restored to the church and its environs, and if the liturgical community were "taught" to understand itself as part of the community of lives memorialized in those burial places, then surely we would more readily see that *every* shout in praise of God, *every* alleluia, is *always* made at the grave. And that is how it ought to be.

Chapter Eleven

Preaching and the Potential of Liturgical Space

Anyone who has ever read a copy of a sermon they had heard preached sometime before, knows that the typescript does not recreate the original experience of hearing the sermon. The power and vitality of the sermon are difficult to re-constitute from the printed page, even for the most imaginative reader. The sermon, delivered in the liturgical context, is composed of the written word, certainly, but it is conveyed

or accomplished by breath, voice, gesture, posture, glance, intonation, location. All these are connected to the event itself and are lost from the sermon "copy," save in the imagination.

Patricia Wilson-Kastner approaches this fact in this way. In her fine insightful book *Imagery for Preaching*, she writes, "Rooted in the liturgy, preaching shares in [the eucharistic liturgy's] visible, tangible, sensory character."[1] Visible, tangible, sensory. Indeed! Preaching is by its very nature an embodied act, a physical part of our common ritual life. The written text is no more fully descriptive of the sermon than the formulas in the Prayer Book are exhaustive of the Sunday morning liturgy. Though we have tried over the years to separate rite and ceremony, sermon and delivery, surely we know they are integral to each other.

In addition to being something physical and embodied, preaching also "takes place." That is, preaching has about it not only physicality but also spatiality.[2]

This combination is the concern of what follows. We shall explore the physical and spatial dimensions of Christian proclamation, taking the gathered eucharistic community as the normative setting. In this exploration, our intent is to consider how the liturgical environment can be used to enhance preaching.

Spatiality

As Marion Hatchett has taught us, the design of the liturgical space in our day is, and must be, informed by the architectural expectations of the liturgy itself.[3] The first necessity imposed on the design of such a space has two facets. First, consideration must be given to the location of the three liturgical centers in association with which the liturgical action is accomplished. These three centers, or better "places," are marked by their own particular ritual object—the font marks the place for initiation, the altar/table marks the place for "Holy Communion" and the ambo (pulpit, lectern) identifies the place for "the Word of God."

A second facet of the design process is determining the shape of the room, the configuration of the several centers and other constituent elements so that seeing and hearing are available to all. Obviously the location of the liturgical centers should influence the shape of the room, rather than the other way around. In addition, the ecclesiology of the Prayer Book being what it is, the shape of the liturgical room ought to make possible some measure of face-to-face access for the congregation. Though actually sitting around a table is not critically important to the point, Rudolf Arnheim is surely right in saying, "When people face one another across a table they testify to their convivial status, that is, to their 'living together' for the occasion. The audience in the usual theater or lecture hall possesses a mere parallelism of purpose and target, which is quite different from doing things *with* other people."[4]

Perhaps, by now, it is not necessary to say more about the appropriateness of "gatheredness" in the design of our liturgical rooms. Nor perhaps is it necessary to argue the appropriateness of reading the Bible and preaching the sermon from the same place. It seems increasingly common in new churches for the ambo to replace the older combination of lectern and pulpit. In such a room, the single ambo would suggest that the reading and preaching done in that place are constituent elements of the same proclamation. The visual or spatial integrity and unity of the proclamation, of course, would depend on the way in which the proclamation space was actually used.

At issue here is a sense of place, and the potential conflict between the spatial signals of "emplacement" and the physical or embodied evidence. It is not uncommon in the Episcopal Church to experience the various aspects of proclamation—readings, psalmody and preaching—occurring at different locations throughout the room. The ambo, as a single place of proclamation, would gather all these up, *if* the ambo were so used. Sadly, in many congregations, wherever the reading and psalmody may occur, the preaching is done in a place-less fashion. This "no-place" is often the altar rail gate, the chancel step or the head of the central aisle. Preaching from "no-place" seems to encourage physical wandering, the kind of aimlessness mirrored far too often in the sermon itself. Preaching from "no-place" gives to preaching an occasional, transient character that hardly dignifies the Word of God.

Those who do this kind of preaching in the ordered liturgy of the church are apparently seeking not only a more conversational style but also more access and intimacy with the congregation. To the extent that such qualities are desirable for proclamation, having to seek for them in "no-place" is a clear judgment on the design of the room itself, testimony to the failure of the design to serve the liturgy.

This raises then the matter of the location of the ambo. What the Prayer Book holds up for the church in the Holy Eucharist is the clear conviction and expectation that the eucharistic rite is composed of two constituent parts, the Word of God and Holy Communion, and that these two parts associated with their respective ritual object, are *of equal value and power in the rite*. From this we can argue that the ritual objects ought to be placed in the room in such a fashion as to show forth this mutuality and interrelationship. Unfortunately, what the Prayer Book sets out in the Holy Eucharist has yet to find spatial expression in the Episcopal Church. Instead of mutuality and reciprocity between the objects and what they signal, we continue to build rooms in which the one object dominates the other, i.e., the altar/table is typically central and the ambo is typically not. This circumstance is no doubt due in great measure to the residual dominance of a particular historical and architectural tradition aided by teachings growing out of the eucharistic reawakening of which the Prayer Book itself is a part. To speak of the church as being eucharistically centered often gets translated into buildings that are altar centered. In contrast, what the Prayer Book teaches, as we have suggested already, is that a eucharistically centered room would have as its focus a pair of objects, ambo and altar/table, which *together* signal the unity of the Word and Holy Communion, at least to those with "eyes to see."

What we are proposing is that the ambo and altar/table be placed in the room in a mutually central place, neither being dominant over the other, neither in fact being on the central axis of the room. What would be central would be the pair, their mutuality, their balance being clearly set forth. This would mean they would share a common elevation and a common platform. Since they would have different volumes, they would need to be placed and proportioned appropriately in order to balance. This would probably mean that one would likely be forward of the other, each on its own side of the central axis. Symmetry, per se, is not the issue, balance is.

Such a "place" would be the normative place for proclamation—readings, psalmody, preaching. Such a place would be the location from which the church would rightly and habitually expect to hear the Word of God.

Physicality

The proclamation of the Word of God requires location. Indeed, it requires a sense of place such as to show forth the intimate relation of proclamation to the visible words enacted in the church's sacraments. So we have argued. In so doing, we have advocated a norm such that the various aspects of proclamation would occur from the same place of prominence and dignity.

We need now to move in another direction. From *emplacement,* we move to *embodiment.* To accomplish this move, we return to the work of Patricia Wilson-Kastner, with whom we began.

Dr. Wilson-Kastner writes very ably about the necessity of imagery for powerful preaching. Early on she says,

> Of particular importance to preachers is the growing recognition that verbal, abstract expression is the province of a few, whereas the visual, sensory and imagery-filled discourse is accessible to virtually everyone. This fact does not mean that preaching is only about the physical world or is confined to what we say and hear. But effective preaching is rooted and focused in the physical and sensory.[5]

Later, she adds,

> . . . the imagery in a sermon encompasses the verbal descriptions and evocations of the visual, tactile, auditory and all other dimensions of the physical world.[6]

Surely, she is right. Effective, persuasive preaching requires the union of rational and sensory-affective dimensions of human knowing. Physicality and embodiment are constitutive of human being. In our preaching the more seriously we take our embodiment the more effective will be our proclamation. As one ponders this insight and is persuaded of its truth, the more one is drawn, ineluctably, into reflections on the physical act of preaching itself.

One of the joys of our liturgical tradition and especially our current liturgical texts is their remarkable combination of stability and variation.

Obviously, it is the nature of the liturgy to be repetitive, creating a stability into which the community enters when it gathers, being formed and reformed as the Body of Christ. For many this stability, predictability and familiarity provide a most powerful place of access to God and God's graciousness. In the presumed "safety" of this stability, we allow ourselves to be vulnerable to the Holy One. The formative influence of the liturgy is keenly experienced through the stability of the liturgy.

Yet, the "ordinary" part of the liturgy is enriched and enlivened by things "proper" to the day or season. In this fashion the vitality of God's companionship to us is re-counted in varied ways, the church year being the principal instrument directing our attention. The cadence of the church year is sufficiently methodical and its impact sufficiently subtle that this variety is welcome and nourishing, rather than disruptive and threatening.[7]

The combination of stability and variety is common to our liturgical life. Together these two protect us from becoming static, on the one hand, or being rootless, on the other. Together they engage our humanity more fully and provide us a richer experience of the presence and intention of God.

The impact of the calendar on preaching is obvious and very important. As mediated through the lectionary, the "stuff" of the calendar becomes the "stuff" of the church's proclamation. It is the calendar (lectionary) that provides focus, support and direction for the proclamation. The lectionary makes our preaching "timely," and therefore rich and varied.[8]

Now if we add to this notion of "timeliness" an increased attention to the sensory-affective dimension of human being and knowing, we come to some interesting possibilities, adventurous suggestions about the proclamation. All of these suggestions grow out of the conviction that the physicality of preaching can be intensified in a timely way, and that doing so will add to the vitality of the homiletical life of the church.

Imagine for the moment that the parish liturgy committee was about the work of planning the services for a particular day or season. In such a setting it would be appropriate and hardly surprising that questions arise about themes and emphases, and about how these themes might be carried out or expressed liturgically. More surprising, however, would be the questions we would urge upon this group. In addition to questions about the way the liturgy should carry the theme, we might ask: How shall we preach? That is, given that the proclamation is the church's proclamation, on this day or season, what shall we say and how shall we say it? These are likely to be new questions for both preacher and liturgy committee, but in our current exploration they are appropriate questions. How shall we "say" our preaching?

Once given permission to wonder about this, or being persuaded that imagining an answer to this question has integrity, it is difficult to know what sort of faithful answer might be forthcoming. It might only be limited by the amount of energy God's Spirit was willing to invest in the enterprise!

Some examples. During seasons in which movement toward a destination is characteristic and integral to the spirituality of things, the preaching might be done so as to intensify that sense of movement. Preaching from "stations," as it were, set in a sequence toward some particular destination could add genuine power to the keeping of the season. If, for instance, in a parish preparing a group of catechumens for baptism at the Easter Vigil, preparation in which the congregation had an obvious investment and involvement, then the stational sermons might "progress" toward the font. This would mark the journey of all the baptized, which is soon to be replicated by the catechumens. This kind of preaching would be a largely verbal exercise enlivened by intentional progressive movement.

Another set of possibilities would involve the reduction of spoken language in favor of other "language" forms. In this group of ideas, the spoken words would be at most the companion or servant of this other "language." Among the examples of this kind, the first and most dramatic would be the use of mime as a vehicle for proclamation. Here, no spoken words would occur at all, save *perhaps* the reading of the text. At the same time, if the pantomime were the "reading" and the "sermon," then silence (or music) would be all that was heard. This physical visualization would carry to fullest expression the line of reasoning set loose by Patricia Wilson-Kastner as we have appropriated it. The "sermon" would be *wholly* "visual, sensory and image filled."[9]

A second kind of less verbal form for preaching would be exemplified by the combination of art or music and words. Careful collaboration between speaker (preacher) and visual artist or musician could yield wonderful results. The contrast between abstract verbal expressions and music, between the externality of even powerful verbal imagery and the engulfing character of music could certainly be integrated into proclamation in rewarding ways. Any sermon aimed to treat matters of harmony and discord might be well served by a "score" to accompany the "libretto" provided by the reading. Even a story like the Prodigal could be faithfully scripted and scored so as to edify the congregation. What a challenge it would be to the musician to score a part for the older brother, surely the "everyman/everywoman" of the parable!

Likewise, the careful working together of a preacher and visual artist could yield equally powerful results. Whether the artist works toward something representational or abstract, whether the artist's work is created "on the spot" or beforehand, line and color can convey as surely as music the sinews and texture of proclamation. This writer has seen this approach used in a strong and captivating way, wherein the artist and preacher did the textual exegesis and hermeneutical preparation together until each and both had what they called an "aha!" The "aha" then became the matter for proclamation in the liturgy. The artist and preacher worked simultaneously and the words and the art piece concluded at the same time, making the same point.

Depending on how these two methods are handled, either can serve as a useful form of proclamation for children, who, one hopes, find themselves more and more a part of the eucharistic community. This would also hold true for mime and for any combination of physical action and words.

Again using personal experience, this writer once "preached" on Luke 13:20, the parable in which the reign of God is said to be "like leaven."

The preacher accomplished the sermon by doing very little speaking but by investing considerable energy in mixing bread dough. The mixing was done in the "crossing" of the building. The speaking that was done, was done by a "baker" who struggled with the dough. What little that was said, spoke of the uncontrollable nature of yeast. "There is in this dough of mine a trickster, a mysterious living power set loose . . . which will change what I plan, what I imagine. It is beyond my control. It works its own work, in spite of me." Such is leaven and the reign of God. Most of what occurred in the "sermon" was visual and physical, and one hopes it was also edifying. (The bread was subsequently baked and eaten.)

To these kinds of examples could certainly be added the often illuminating effects of drama. As exposition and elaboration of a text, drama can be a good preacher and evangelist. The same is true of liturgical dance. Yet another option might be variations of the dialogue sermon in which several speakers are involved, perhaps located at various points in the room. This might be an effective way to stage a debate between Jesus and his detractors or to narrate sections of Job.

Certainly this list and these examples could be expanded greatly. However, in all these examples and any other as well, it is crucial that the "staging" be done with great care, the same care as the rest of the liturgy. If any of these methods were employed, speaking now in minimal terms, the people must tolerate it, the space available must tolerate it and certainly the "preacher" must tolerate it. Only these working in concert will prove fertile ground for proclamation.

Ordinary and Proper

In conclusion, we need to gather up the concern of the first part of this essay and the concern of the second. Early on we advocated the spatial union of the aspects of proclamation (reading, psalmody, preaching) into a single "place." This place, the ambo, was offered as the *normative* location for proclamation, clearly preferable to visual fragmentation of the readings and to preaching from "no-place." In the second section, we have suggested that preaching take a more physical form and take on a spatial expression that makes more expansive use of the liturgical space.

In order to reconcile these two apparently contradictory ideas, we need to return to the interplay of "ordinary" and "proper," an interplay focused by the issue of timeliness. Simply put, if the norm is well fixed, then timely variations from it have their "place" and can be profoundly effective and powerful. This would mean that the ambo would be the "ordinary" place, and an oration would be the "ordinary" style. Such would be the typical, predictable and expected norm. However, variations in a timely, "proper" fashion could occur. Without the solid support and foundation of the norm, timeliness is exchanged for chaos, and the community of the faithful is not edified nor is God glorified. "Seasoning" the norm brings to it remarkable vitality.

---

1. (Philadelphia: Fortress Press, 1989), p. 14.

2. Regarding the matter of "place," the following might be useful: Kent C. Bloomer and Charles W. Moore, *Body, Memory and Architecture* (Yale, 1977); Christian Norberg-Schulz, *The Concept of Dwelling* (New York: Rizzoli, 1985); and Jonathan Z. Smith, *To Take Place* (Chicago: The University of Chicago, 1987).

3. "The Architectural Implications of the Book of Common Prayer," (New York: Standing Liturgical Commission, 1984), Occasional Paper Number 7.

4. *The Dynamics of Architectural Form* (Berkeley, CA: The University of California Press, 1977), p. 269.

5. *Imagery for Preaching,* p. 13.

6. *Ibid.,* p. 48.

7. On the impact of the church year, see Christopher Kiesling, "The Formative Influence of Liturgy," in *Studies in Formative Spirituality,* III/3 (November, 1982).

8. Some of what follows is dependent on flexible or variable liturgical space. On this subject see my article, "An Apology for Variable Liturgical Space," in *Worship* 61/3 (May, 1987). It is also a chapter in the present volume.

9. *Imagery for Preaching,* previously cited, p. 13.

Afterword

At the beginning of this collection, I confessed to having had some second or third thoughts about some things. It's time to report.

First, as regards the matter of variable liturgical space, the essay contained here was first read to a gathering of liturgical teachers and practitioners at a meeting of the Environment and Art Study Group of the North American Academy of Liturgy. Several members of the group had received advance copies of my paper and were asked to comment. The respondents, Andrew Ciferni, O. Praem., James F. White and S. Anita Stauffer, were generally supportive of the intent and general direction of the material and thought the ideas worth setting loose in some broader way than just our discussion group. And, of course, each of them had something to say to extend or broaden or challenge my suggestions.

The concern raised most clearly by Anita Stauffer is the one that has stimulated rather continuous reflection on my part. It was my contention in the essay that *all* the furniture in the liturgical setting ought to permit variation, including the baptismal font. Anita's conviction was that an authentic baptismal theology required a font of such proportions that portability would be (and should be) impossible. That the font would actually be a pool, and that the pool would be continuously filled with water—these realities would preclude varying the font's location. There were others in the group, Frank Kacmarcik in particular, who were similarly persuaded.

I find myself now *nearly* of the same opinion. My hesitation is not really at the level of principle but rather at the level of practice. That is, for Episcopal congregations, these two ideas—fonts as pools and variable liturgical space—come as fundamental challenges to "the way we've always done it." In my conversations with congregations, the idea of either a baptismal pool or designing and building a variable space usually causes anxiety, shortness of breath or a tolerant and dismissive smile.

In this situation, I would happily settle for the acceptance of either as a faithful articulation for liturgical design—a pool in a fixed room, or a sizable but movable font in a variable room. The likelihood of persuading a congregation or committee of the virtues of a pool, fixed and full, in an otherwise variable room takes *my* breath away!

In any event, I am certainly persuaded of the need for a formidable baptismal font, be it a pool or otherwise. And I would advocate such with much vigor and conviction, with more vigor and conviction, in fact, than I would mobilize in favor of variable space. I would want the water to win, if it came to a contest with variety.

A second change of heart or mind has to do with the exchange of the peace in the eucharistic liturgy. In the current collection and in *Shaped by Images,* I speak about the exchange of the peace being done with a certain ritual restraint, something that contrasts markedly with the unrestrained character that sometimes typifies this liturgical moment in some congregations. I have been willing to admit and rejoice in the social character of the moment but have tended to advocate a kind of discipline to this exchange which would conform its *temper* to the typically modest temper of the rest of the liturgy. My assumption here, I discover, is that the "temper of the rest of the liturgy" is generally without much energy, enthusiasm or "personality." It's as if the peace needs to feel like the German hymns feel!

My own evolution is teaching me more about this, week by week. With my life companion, I attend a parish where the *temper* of the liturgy tends to be congruent throughout, a principle about which I am pleased. At the same time, the *temper* of St. James' Church in Austin, Texas, does *not* feel like a German hymn, though sing them we do. What I discover is that congruence can be served very well when the level of energy is very high as well as under other circumstances.

These two matters, the variable font question and the congruence of the peace, have experienced some substantial review over time, review that might cause me to rewrite some of what I have said in these essays and elsewhere. Beyond these matters, however, there is something dawning in my consciousness that would invite fundamental rethinking at a number of points. It deserves a mention.

Over the last year or two, I have found myself in a number of conversations, both in class and out, about the canon which reads "No unbaptized person shall be eligible to receive Holy Communion in this church" (Title I, Canon 17, section 7). I have a variety of feelings and reactions to this canon and the assorted issues it sets loose. [There is much to say about this matter and I do not want to treat it too briskly or superficially, but the underpinnings of an opinion come rather readily to mind.]

First of all, the canon seems an odd rendering of the implications of the invitation that often reads, "All baptized persons are welcome to receive Holy Communion at St. Anne's." The intended generosity of this invitation is clearly stripped away in the language of the canon. "The Episcopal Church Does Not Welcome You!"

Secondly, and I have been helped here by Richard Fabian and Andrew Doyle, I wonder what hermeneutic we might mobilize to interpret this canon in light of Jesus' directive to feed the hungry. If someone—unwashed—comes to the table where there is food and they are hungry, what are we to do? I cannot see a faithful way of turning them away.

Hospitality and faithfulness would be my avenues into a nuanced investigation of the consequences of this proscriptive canon. They would also be my entries into the question of the admission of *everyone/anyone* to the altar/table.

To conclude, I find myself increasingly startled at the extent to which we Episcopalians need to control liturgical things, things which might flourish if left alone, things which ought not to invite control at all. Recently, I received a packet of information from the most recent meeting of a diocesan liturgy and music commission. In it, I read of an extended discussion on limiting the number of trained lay eucharistic visitors a congregation could license. I thought to myself, this ministry is fundamental to hospitality, evangelism and Christian nurture; it is the clear practice of the ancient church, and we are debating and *wanting to control* how many people ought to do it?! I felt amazement, sorrow and anger in equal measure.

All of this is to say that things change and the changes need to have their way with us. My own thinking is clearly in process, moving somewhere, like the furniture. I am eager to see where it goes.